D1713872

A COMMENTARY
ON TEXTUAL ADDITIONS TO
THE NEW TESTAMENT

A COMMENTARY
ON TEXTUAL ADDITIONS TO
THE NEW TESTAMENT

PHILIP WESLEY COMFORT

Kregel
Academic

A Commentary on Textual Additions to the New Testament
© 2017 by Philip Wesley Comfort

Published by Kregel Publications, a division of Kregel, Inc., 2450 Oak Industrial Dr. NE, Grand Rapids, MI 49505-6020.

Nestle-Aland, Novum Testamentum Graece, 28th Revised Edition, edited by Barbara and Kurt Aland, Johannes Karavidopoulos, Carlo M. Martini, and Bruce M. Metzger in cooperation with the Institute for New Testament Textual Research, Münster/Westphalia, © 2012 Deutsche Bibelgesellschaft, Stuttgart. Used by permission.

The translation of the New Testament portions used throughout the commentary is the author's own English rendering of the Greek.

The Hebrew font NewJerusalemU and the Greek font GraecaU are available from www.linguistsoftware.com/lgku.htm, +1-425-775-1130.

ISBN 978-0-8254-4509-5

Printed in the United States of America
17 18 19 20 21 / 5 4 3 2 1

Contents

Introduction

Jesus was famous for speaking in parables. One parable he told was as follows: "The kingdom of heaven is like yeast that a woman took and mixed with three measures of dough until the whole was leavened" (Matt 13:33). Unleavened bread is flat and thin; leavened bread is puffed up and full. This is a good illustration of what happened to the New Testament text. Throughout the history of textual transmission, the text grew larger by scribal additions. Many verses were added to the text as found in Matthew 6:13b; 7:13; 12:47; 16:2–4; 17:21; 18:11; 21:44; 23:14; 26:49–50; Mark 7:16; 9:44, 46; 11:26; 15:28; 16:9–20: Luke 9:54–56; 17:36; 22:43–44; 23:17, 34a: John 5:3b–4; 7:53–8:11; 9:38–39; 13:23; Acts 8:37; 15:34; 24:6a-8; 28:29; Romans 11:6b; 14:6b; 16:24; Galatians 1:9; 1:15b; Colossians 2:2b; 1 Thessalonians 1:1a; Hebrews 2:7b; 3:6b; 11:37a; 1 Peter 5:14b; 1 John 4:3b; 5:7a–8a; and Revelation 1:18b; 20:5a. In addition, many phrases and words were added, which are too numerous to list here but will be covered in this book.

The Greek edition known as the Textus Receptus, current in the fifteenth and sixteenth century, has thousands more words than the primitive text presented in the manuscripts of the second through fourth centuries. Major English translations of the 1500s and 1600s such as Tyndale's New Testament and the King James Version, based on the Textus Receptus, have all these extra verses, phrases, and words. Those who read the King James Version (also the New King James Version) are reading a "leavened" version—that is, it is a text with thousands of extra words.

The aim of this book is to show these additions in a manner that is clear to English readers, and then explain why they were added. But before we look at the individual verses, we need to explore the reasons why the additions took place in the New Testament text. In short, the additions were the result of scribal gap-filling wherein scribes added words as they read and copied a text. The sources for the additions came from their own minds, other gospels, other scriptures, and oral traditions. We know that these were additions when we do the practice of textual criticism—the science and art of determining which reading (among many in the various manuscripts) is most likely the original reading and which reading or readings are variants.

Most modern textual critics use one rule-of-thumb or "canon" as they go about doing the task of recovering the original wording of the text. They try to abide by the rule that the reading that is most likely original is the one that best explains the variants. This canon is actually a development of a maxim proposed by Bengel in *Gnomon Novi Testamenti* wherein he said, *proclivi scriptoni praestat ardua* ("the harder reading is to be preferred"), a maxim he formulated in responding to his own question as to which variant reading is likely to have arisen out of the others.

This overarching canon for internal criticism involves several criteria, which one scholar or another has posited and/or implemented during the past three hundred years of New Testament textual criticism. Having made a thorough historical survey of the development of canons for internal criticism, Epp ("The Eclectic Method in New Testament Textual Criticism: Solution or Symptom?" *Harvard Theological Review* 69 (1976), 243) summarized all the criteria as follows:

1. A variant's status as the shorter or shortest reading
2. A variant's status as the harder or hardest reading
3. A variant's fitness to account for the origin, development, or presence of all other readings
4. A variant's conformity to the author's style and vocabulary
5. A variant's conformity to the author's theology or ideology
6. A variant's conformity to Koine (rather than Attic) Greek
7. A variant's conformity to Semitic forms of expression

8. A variant's lack of conformity to parallel passages or to extraneous items in its context generally
9. A variant's lack of conformity to Old Testament passages
10. A variant's lack of conformity to liturgical forms and usages
11. A variant's lack of conformity to extrinsic doctrinal views

It should be admitted that some of these criteria are problematic when implemented. Two textual critics, using the same principle to examine the same variant unit, will not agree. For example, with respect to the fourth criterion, one critic will argue that one variant was produced by a copyist attempting to emulate the author's style; the other will claim the same variant has to be original because it accords with the author's style. And with respect to the fifth criterion, one will argue that one variant was produced by an orthodox scribe attempting to rid the text of a reading that could be used to promote heterodoxy or heresy; another will claim that the same variant has to be original because it is orthodox and accords with Christian doctrine (thus a heterodoxical or heretical scribe must have changed it).

Furthermore, internal criticism allows for the possibility that the reading selected for the text can be taken from any manuscript of any date. This produces subjective eclecticism. Those who advocate "thoroughgoing eclecticism" have argued for the legitimacy of certain variant readings on the basis of internal criticism alone. The readings they favor do have some manuscript support, but often it comes from one Latin version (versus all Greek witnesses), or a late minuscule, or the testimony of some church father. Modern textual scholars try to temper the subjectivism by employing a method called "reasoned eclecticism." According to Holmes, "Reasoned eclecticism applies a combination of internal and external considerations, evaluating the character of the variants in light of the MSS evidence and vice versa in order to obtain a balanced view of the matter and as a check upon purely subjective tendencies" ("New Testament Textual Criticism." *Introducing New Testament Interpretation*, 53).

I would argue that scribal-gap filling needs to be added to the canon of textual criticism. Any textual variant that appears to fill in a gap in the text is suspect as a scribal emendation. This covers three of the criteria described above and goes beyond them: (1) the shortest reading is to preferred, (2) the hardest reading is to be preferred, (3) the reading that shows scribal harmonization to a parallel passage (especially in the Gospels) is suspect as a scribal harmonization. Thus, the new canon should state that a reading which appears to be the result of scribal gap-filling should be regarded as a variant from the original text.

Scribal gap-filling accounts for many of the textual variants (especially textual expansions) in the New Testament—particularly in the narrative books (the four gospels and Acts), but also in all the other books. Usually, textual critics examine textual variants as accidental deviations from the original text. However, some variants may be accounted for more accurately as individual "reader-receptions" of the text. By this, I mean variants were created by individual scribes as they interpreted the text in the process of reading it. In the centuries prior to the production of copies via dictation (wherein many scribes in a scriptorium transcribed a text as it was dictated to them by one reader), all manuscript copies were made singly—each scribe working alone to produce a copy from an exemplar. The good scribe was expected not to have really processed the text internally but to have mechanically copied it word by word, even letter by letter. But no matter how meticulous or professional, a scribe would become subjectively involved with the text and—whether consciously or unconsciously—at times produce a transcription that differed from his exemplar, thereby leaving a written legacy of his individual reading of the text.

Even a scribe as meticulous as the one who produced $\mathfrak{P}^{75}$ could not refrain, on occasion, from filling in a perceived gap. This occurs in the parable in Luke 16:19–31 where the reader is told of an unnamed rich man and a beggar who has a name, Lazarus. Perceiving a gap in the story, the scribe gives the rich man a name: "Neues," perhaps meaning "Nineveh" (see note on Luke 16:19). Other scribes gave names to the two unnamed revolutionaries crucified with Jesus: Zoatham and Camma (in some manuscripts), or Joathas and Maggatras (in other manuscripts). Many other scribes filled in bigger gaps, especially in narratives. One example comes to mind in the story of the salvation of the Ethiopian eunuch recorded in Acts 8:26–40, wherein some scribes added an entire verse so as to fill in a perceived gap of what one must confess before being baptized. Thus, we are given these extra words in Acts 8:37, "And Philip said, 'If you believe with all your heart, you may [be baptized].' And he [the eunuch] replied, 'I believe that Jesus Christ is the Son of God.'" (See the note on Acts 8:37 for further discussion.)

The observations of certain literary theorists who focus on reader-reception theory help us understand the dynamic interaction between the scribe (functioning as a true reader) and the text he or she was copying. Textual critics must take into account the historical situation of the scribes who produced the manuscripts we rely on for textual criticism. Textual critics must also realize that scribes were interactive readers. Indeed, as many literary critics in recent years have shifted their focus from the text itself to the readers of the text in an attempt to comprehend plurality of interpretation, so textual critics could analyze variant readings in the textual tradition as possibly being the products of different, personalized "readings" of the text created by the scribes who produced them.

The work of Wolfgang Iser is useful for understanding how scribes read and processed a text as they transcribed it. Iser is concerned not just with the question of what a literary text makes its readers do but with how readers participate in creating meaning. In other words, the meaning of a text is not inherent in the text but must be actualized by the reader. A reader must act as cocreator of the text by supplying that portion of it which is not written but only implied. Each reader uses his or her imagination to fill in the unwritten portions of the text, its "gaps" or areas of "indeterminacy." In other words, the meaning of a text is gradually actualized as the reader adopts the perspectives thrust on him or her by the text, experiences it sequentially, has expectations frustrated or modified, relates one part of the text to the other, and imagines and fills in all that the text leaves blank. The reader's reflection on the thwarting of his or her expectations, the negations of familiar values, the causes of their failure, and whatever potential solutions the text offers require the reader to take an active part in formulating the meaning of the narrative.

Whereas readers do this gap-filling in their imaginations only, scribes sometimes took the liberty to fill the unwritten gaps with written words. In other words, some scribes went beyond just imagining how the gaps should be filled and actually filled them. The historical evidence shows that each scribe who copied a text created a new written text. Although there are many factors that could have contributed to the making of this new text, one major factor is that the text constantly demands the reader to fill in the gaps.

The observations of certain literary theorists, who focused on reader-reception theory, help us understand the dynamic interaction between the scribe (functioning as a true reader) and the text he or she was copying. Each scribe had his own "horizon of expectation" for the text as he read it and produced a copy—an observation noted especially by Gadamer (see bibliography). That horizon for New Testament scribes was formed by their knowledge of the other gospels, other scriptures, Christian theology, and oral traditions. In other words, the scribe copying Matthew had Mark, Luke, and John in mind as he copied Matthew. If a reading in the Gospel of Matthew did not replicate the other gospels, the scribe made the change accordingly to harmonize Matthew to the other gospels. I doubt scribes actually took the time to look up a parallel passage, but just naturally made a change from their memorized knowledge of the Gospels.

A literary work is not autonomous but is an intensional object that depends on the cognition of the reader. As an intensional object, a literary work cannot fill in all the details; the reader is required to do this. During the reading process, the reader must concretize the gaps by using his or her imagination to give substance to textual omission and/or indefiniteness. Since this substantiation is a subjective and creative act, the concretization will assume many variations for different readers. For example, the Gospel of Luke says that the crowds who had watched Jesus' crucifixion "returned home, beating their breasts" (Luke 23:48). Although it would seem that most readers are given enough text to visualize this scene, the imagination of various scribes was sparked to consider how extensive their grief was or to recreate what they might have been saying to one another as they walked home. A few scribes, imagining a more intense reaction, added, "they returned home, beating their breasts *and foreheads.*" Other scribes provided some dialogue: "they returned home beating their breasts, *and saying, 'Woe to us for the sins we have committed this day, for the destruction of Jerusalem is imminent!'*"

Iser calls the textual gaps "blanks"; each blank is a nothing that propels communication because the blank requires an act of ideation in order to be filled. "Blanks suspend connectibility of textual patterns, the resultant break in good continuation intensifies the acts of ideation on the reader's part, and in this respect the blank functions as an elementary function of communication" (*The Act of Reading*, 1978, 189) According to Iser, the central factor in literary communication concerns the reader's filling in of these textual blanks. His theory of textual gaps is useful for understanding scribal reader-reception. Of course, his perception of gaps or blanks is usually far bigger and more demanding on the reader's imaginative powers than was usually the case for New Testament scribes. Nonetheless, scribes were confronted with gaps or blanks that begged for imaginative filling. Many scribes, when confronted with such textual gaps, took the liberty to fill in those gaps by adding extra words or changing the wording to provide what they thought would be a more communicative text. Indeed, the entire history of New Testament textual transmission shows the text getting longer and longer due to textual interpolations—i.e., the filling in of perceived gaps. We especially see the work of gap-filling in the narrative portions of the New Testament, Gospels and Acts. Substantial number of expansions in the D-text in Acts are the work of editorialization, not exactly scribal gap-filling. I have commented on every addition in my book, *New Testament Text and Translation Commentary* (325–433). In this volume I will comment only on those additions that are the result of the act of reading and that have been filled by several MSS (which may sometimes include D).

Textual critics judge textual variants as being scribal creations if they appear to be the result of harmonization from one gospel to another. For example, Matthew 9:13 reads, "I [Jesus] have not come to call the righteous but sinners," according to early and good manuscripts. Other manuscripts complete the thought by adding the words "to repentance." Thus, this becomes, "I [Jesus] have not come to call the righteous but sinners to repentance." Textual critics will be quick to point out that this addition was made by way of a harmonization to Luke 5:32, a parallel passage. While that may be true, I do not think the scribe stopped his copying process, looked up Luke 5:32, and then made the addition. Rather, the scribe having read Luke had this passage in his mind and thereby it formed his horizon of expectation. So when he was copying Matthew and didn't see "to repentance," he thought it and then added it. Or, he could have not been thinking of the parallel passage in Luke at all and just simply completed the grammatical gap of "I have not come to call"—call to what?—and so a scribe added "to repentance."

In the final analysis, I would say that scribal gap-filling accounts for many textual variants in the gospel narratives. Some textual critics will say that this is nothing more than rote harmonization. This is true to a certain extent. But I don't think scribes did a thoroughgoing harmonization of one gospel to another, by actually checking one with another by taking the time on a verse- by-verse basis to make sure the Gospels or other scriptures harmonized. Rather, scribes having the Gospels memorized just harmonized one gospel to another in the process of acting as real readers of the text. In other words, the reading in one gospel formed their horizon of expectation for their reading of the gospel they were reading and copying, and when they sensed a gap, they filled it accordingly.

Scribes also made additions from oral traditions. This occurred with the so-called "bloody sweat passage" in Luke 22:43–44, wherein it is added that Jesus was praying so hard that his sweat turned to blood and then angels ministered to him. This also occurred in Luke 23:34, wherein an addition has the crucified Jesus saying, "Father, forgive them because they do not know what they are doing." And it happened in John 7:53–8:11, wherein the story of the woman caught in adultery then forgiven and saved by Jesus was added. These and other additions that came from oral tradition will be discussed in this book at length.

Almost all of these additions became part of the Majority Text, or what is also known as the Textus Receptus, from which the New Testament of the King James Version was translated. Long story short: The King James Version contains virtually all the scribal additions noted in this book. This amounts to thousands of added words.

Chapter One

The Gospel of Matthew

Matthew
1:16 | (added words in bold)
The father of Joseph, the husband of **the virgin** Mary, of whom Jesus was born, who is called Christ.

Original Text: Ιωσηφ τον ανδρα Μαριας, εξ ης εγεννηθη Ιησους (**Joseph the husband of Mary, of whom was born Jesus**). This is the original reading according to early and diverse manuscript support ($\mathfrak{P}^1$ ℵ B C L W f 1 33 Maj).
Textual Gap-filling: Some scribe or scribes (Θ f^{13} it), influenced by their knowledge of Mary or influenced by the context (1:23), added παρθενος (virgin) to "Mary" so as to make it clear that this was a virgin birth. Once ancient MS (syr^s) reads: "Joseph, to whom Mary a virgin was betrothed, was the father of Jesus." This translation could be taken to mean that Jesus was not born of a virgin (see NEBmg NJBmg), but it could just as well be a scribal attempt to make it clear that Joseph was the legal father of Jesus.

2:18 | (added words in bold)
A voice was heard in Ramah, **weeping**, wailing, and mourning, Rachel weeping for her children.

Original Text: κλαυθμος και οδυρμος πολυς (**wailing and great mourning**). The original wording "wailing and great mourning" is found in the earliest MSS (א B) and Z.

Textual Gap-filling: Some scribe (perhaps the scribe of W) added και θρενος (and weeping) to make it "wailing and weeping and great mourning" (C D L W 0233 Maj) because his horizon of expectation was formed by Jeremiah 31:15 LXX, the verse quoted here. Subsequent copyists carried on the expansion. The addition is in the TR and KJV.

3:11 | (added words in bold)
The one coming **after me** is more powerful than I am.

Original Text: ο δε ερχομενος (**the one coming, or the coming One**). This is the reading in $\mathfrak{P}^{101}$, the earliest MS. The reference is to Jesus, the Messiah, the coming One.

Textual Gap-filling: The words οπισω μου (after me) were added in א B C D L W 0233. Scribes, having the other gospels as their horizon of expectation, filled in the words οπισω μου (after me): "the one coming after me" (see Mark 1:7; John 1:15).

3:16 | (added words in bold)
The heavens were opened **to him**.

Original Text: ηνεωχθησαν οι ουρανοι (**the heavens were opened**). This is the reading in the earliest MSS, א* B (and Irenaeus, according to a citation of Matthew 3:16–17 in P. Oxy. 405). The earliest extant manuscript that preserves Matthew's record of Jesus' baptism is P. Oxyrhynchus 405, which preserves a portion of Irenaeus' *Against Heresies* (3.9) in which Matthew 3:16–17 is quoted. (The editors of P. Oxy. 405 dated the MS to the late second century. As such, this MS represents a very early copy of Irenaeus' original work, which was produced around AD 150–175.) The account of Jesus' baptism, as recorded in Matthew 3:16–17, is repeated in the course of Irenaeus' argument. A careful transcriptional reconstruction reveals that this manuscript most likely concurs with א and B.

Textual Gap-filling: The word αυτω (to him) was added, as found in later MSS (א¹ Dˢ L W 0233 Maj; so KJV). Since the documentary support for the omission of "to him" is strong (the three earliest MSS), it is likely that a later scribe added "to him" in an attempt to harmonize this part of the verse to 16b, which states that Jesus (not the crowd gathered there) saw God's Spirit descending upon him. It is also possible that scribes harmonized Matthew to Mark (this gospel forming their horizon of expectation), who portrays the baptism as Jesus' private experience (Jesus sees the heavens opened and hears the heavenly voice). But the whole tenor of Matthew's account implies a public unveiling.

4:10 | (added words in bold)
Jesus said to him, "**Get behind** me, Satan."

Original Text: υπαγε (**go away**). This is the original wording in the earliest MSS (א B W).

Textual Gap-filling: This is expanded to υπαγε οπισω μου (get behind me) in later MSS (C² [sixth century] D L 33 Maj; so TR and KJV), by way of scribal conformity to Matt 16:23, a verse that formed a strong horizon of expectation for this verse.

4:12 | (added words in bold)
When **Jesus** heard that John was imprisoned.

Some MSS (C² L W ƒ^1,13 Maj) add ο Ιησους (**Jesus**) at the beginning of the verse. The addition is a reintroduced subject from 4:10. This shows the influence of oral reading on the written text. The same addition occurs in most English versions.

5:11 | (added word in bold)
They speak every evil **word** against you.

Original Text: ειπωσιν παν πονηρον καθ υμων ψευδομενοι (**they speak every evil against you falsely**). This is likely the original wording according to the two earliest MSS (א B).

Textual Gap-filling: The word ρημα (word) was added after "evil" by the scribes of C W Θ 0196 *f* [1,13] Maj as a natural expansion of a scribal filler.

5:25 | (added words in bold)
Lest your accuser hand you over to the judge and the judge **hand you over** to the guard.

Original Text: μηποτε σε παραδω ο αντιδικος τω κριτη, και ο κριτης τω υπηρετν (**lest your accuser hand you over to the judge and the judge to the guard.**) In the second clause, the original wording "and the judge to the guard" is found in the three earliest MSS ($\mathfrak{P}^{64+67}$ ℵ B). **Textual Gap-filling:** This is expanded in the second clause by adding σε παραδω (hand you over), thus the rendering "and the judge hand you over to the guard," as in (D) L W 33 Maj, by way of natural scribal gap-filling. This addition is in the TR and KJV.

5:44a | (added words in bold)
Love your enemy and pray for those who persecute you. **Bless those who curse you, do good to those who hate you.**

Original Text: αγαπατε τους εχθρους υμων (**love your enemies**). The original wording "love your enemies" is found in the two earliest MSS (ℵ B). **Textual Gap-filling:** Some scribes add ευλυγειτε τους καταρωμενους υμας, καλως ποιετε τοις μισουσιν υμας (bless those who curse you, do good to those who hate you), as found in later MSS (D L W 33 Maj; so TR and KJV) This is scribal harmonization to Luke 6:27–28, parallel verses. The text in Luke formed a horizon of expectation for a scribe or scribes, who filled the text in Matthew accordingly.

5:44b | (added words in bold)
Pray for those **who despitefully use you.**

Original Text: προσευχεσθε υπερ των διωκοντων υμας (**pray for the ones persecuting you**). This original wording is found in the two earliest MSS (ℵ B).

Textual Gap-filling: Some scribes add των επηρεαζοντων υμας (the ones despitefully using you), as in later MSS (D L W 33 Maj), by way of scribal harmonization to Luke 6:27–28, parallel verses which formed a strong horizon of expectation. This addition is in the TR and KJV.

6:4 | (added words in bold)
Your Father who sees secretly will reward you **openly.**

Original Text: αποδωσει σοι (**will reward you**). The original wording "reward you" is found in early MSS (א B D W).
Textual Gap-filling: The words εν τω φανερω (in the open) were added by scribes, creating the reading "reward you openly," as found in L W Maj (so TR and KJV). The addition of "in the open" was created by scribes to give antithetical balance to the expression, "in secret."

6:8 | (added words in bold)
God your Father knows what you need.

Original Text: ο πατηρ υμων (**your Father**). The original wording "your Father" is found in several MSS (א* D L W Z 0170[vid] 33 Maj).
Textual Gap-filling: The word θεος (God) was added, creating the reading "God your Father," as found in א[1] B. Since Matthew never elsewhere uses the expression "God your Father," it was probably adapted by scribes who had Paul's epistles as their horizon of expectation and made the expansion accordingly.

6:13 | (added words in bold)
Rescue us from the evil one. **For yours is the kingdom and the power and the glory forever. Amen. [and other alternative additions—see below]**

Original Text: ρυσαι ημας απο του πονηρου (**rescue us from the evil one**). The original prayer ends here in the earliest MSS (א B D Z 0170). One early MS (P. Oxyrhychus 4010) also ends here.

Textual Gap-filling: Scribes felt disappointed with this ending and sensed a gap, so they added a more satisfactory ending. Among other MSS, there are six different additions to the short form of the Lord's Prayer, as follows: (1) add "amen" in 13 Vulgate manuscripts; (2) add "because yours is the power and the glory forever. amen" in cop[sa,fay] (Didache omits amen); (3) add "because yours is the kingdom and the glory forever. amen" in syr[c]; (4) "because yours is the kingdom and the power and the glory forever" in it[k] syr[p]; (5) add "because yours is the kingdom and the power and the glory forever. Amen"—so L W Θ 0233 33 Maj (so TR and KJV); (6) "because yours is the kingdom of the Father and of the Son of and of the sacred Spirit, forever and ever. amen" in 1253 Chrysostom.

These represent the six basic variations of the doxology that were added to the Lord's Prayer. The testimony of the earliest extant witnesses reveals that the prayer must have concluded with a petition for deliverance from evil. The variety among the variants speaks against the genuineness of any of the additions. What is presented above shows the continual expansion of the addition—from the simple "amen" in variant 1 to the elaborate Trinitarian doxology in variant 6. All the variants are scribal gap-fillers, wherein various scribes expected a more satisfactory ending to the most famous prayer in the New Testament and thereby added one.

Though most modern English versions (see NIV and NLT for examples) do not include any of these endings to the Lord's Prayer, the traditional one (found in the KJV) is still repeated by individuals and most churches. The only exception to this that I know of is that Roman Catholic churches conclude the prayer with "rescue us from the evil one." But then the traditional ending is sung.

6:15 | (added words in bold)
If you do not forgive people **their trespasses**.

Original Text: if you do not forgive people. The original wording "forgive people" is found in ℵ D.

Textual Gap-filling: This is expanded by adding τα παραπτωματα αυτων (their trespasses), as in B L D W 33 Maj (so TR and KJV). The addition is a natural scribal expansion supplying just exactly what someone is supposed to forgive another person. In other words, scribes not only thought this as they were reading, they actually added it in writing.

6:18 | (added words in bold)
Your Father who sees secretly rewards you **openly**.

Original Text: αποδωσει σοι (**will reward you**). The original wording "reward you" is found in early MSS (א B D).
Textual Gap-filling: The words εν τω φανερω (in the open) were added by scribes, creating the reading "reward you openly," as found in L W 33 Maj (so TR and KJV). The addition of "in the open" was created by scribes to give antithetical balance to the expression, "in secret."

6:33 | (added words in bold)
First of all pursue the kingdom **of God**.

Original Text: την βασιλειαν (**the kingdom**). This is the original wording according to the earliest MSS (א B).
Textual Gap-filling: The words του θεου (of God) were added, creating the expanded reading, "the kingdom of God," as in L W 0233 33 Maj (so TR and KJV). The scribes' horizon of expectation created this, from their reading of other texts where "kingdom of God" was a more familiar expression.

7:29 | (added words in bold)
He taught them with authority, not like the scribes **and Pharisees**.

Original Text: γραμματεις (**scribes**). This is the original reading according to the two earliest MSS (א B).
Textual Gap-filling: Later MSS (C* W 33) add και οι Φαρισαοι (and the Pharisees)—a natural scribal expansion because "scribes and Pharisees" often appear side by side in the Gospels, thereby creating a horizon of expectation for their reading of this text.

8:13 | (added words in bold)
The servant was healed in that hour. **And the centurion returned to his house that same hour and found his servant healed.**

Original Text: ιαθη ο παις εν τη ωρα εκεινη (**the servant was healed in that hour**). This original wording is found in two early MSS (ℵ[1] B).
Textual Gap-filling: Some scribes added και υποστρεψας ο εκατονταρχος εις τον οικον αυτου εν αυτη τη ωρα ευρεν τον παιδα υγιαινοντα (and the centurion returned to his house that same hour and found his servant healed), as found in ℵ[*,2] C Θ f^1 (33). Some scribe or scribes thought this was the same healing that was recorded in John 4, thereby forming a horizon of expectation for his or their reading of Matthew, and so they added words that were influenced by John 4:52–53. They did not do a rote harmonization from John 4 because the added text in Matthew is not verbatim from John.

8:29 | (added word in bold)
"Jesus, **Son of God**, leave us alone."

Original Text: υιε του θεου (**Son of God**). This is the original wording is found in the early MSS (ℵ B C*), as well as L 33.
Textual Gap-filling: The name Ιησους was added creating the title, "Jesus, Son of God," as found in C[3] [ninth century] W Maj (so TR and KJV), by way of scribal expansion.

9:13 | (added words in bold)
For I have not come to call the righteous but sinners **to repentance.**

Original Text: ου γαρ ηλθον καλεσαι δικαιους αλλα αμαρτωλους (**for I have not come to call the righteous but sinners**). This is the original wording according to excellent testimony (ℵ B D W 0233 33).
Textual Gap-filling: Other MSS (C L Θ 0281 Maj) add εις μετανοιαν (to repentance) to the end of this statement, either by way of scribal harmonization to Luke 5:32 (Luke forming the horizon of expectation for their reading of Matthew) or by way of naturally completing the

thought "I have come to call"—call to what?—which was then filled in by "to repentance." This addition is in the TR and KJV.

9:14 | (added word in bold)
Then John's disciples came to him and asked, "Why do we and the Pharisees fast **often**, but your disciples don't fast?"

Original Text: νηστευομεν (**fast**). The original wording is simply "fast" according to the earliest MSS (ℵ* B).
Textual Gap-filling: One of two words were added here πυκνα, πολλα. Thus, we have "fast frequently" in ℵ¹ and "fast often" in ℵ² [seventh century] C D L W 0233 Maj; so TR and KJV). Both variants appear to be scribal additions intended to make a more effective contrast between the fasting of the Pharisees and John's disciples with the lack thereof on the part of Jesus' disciples. Indeed, many copyists would not want readers thinking that Jesus condemned fasting completely.

10:12 | (added words in bold)
As you enter the house, give it greetings, **saying "peace be to this house."**

Original Text: ασπασασθε αυτην (**greet it**). This is the original wording according to two early MSS (B C).
Textual Gap-filling: Several MSS (ℵ*,² D L W 0281ᵛⁱᵈ) add λεγωντες ειρηνη τω οικω τουτω, ("saying, 'peace to this house')." The addition, though found in a number of witnesses, was probably influenced by Luke 10:5, a parallel passage, by scribes who considered Matthew's wording too terse. Luke formed a horizon of expectation for their reading of Matthew.

12:15 | (added word in bold)
Many **crowds** were coming to hear him.

Original Text: πολλοι (**many**). The two earliest MSS (ℵ B) read this way, thus the rendering, "many were coming to hear him [Jesus]."

Textual Gap-filling: Other MSS add οχλοι (crowds), as in C D L W Θ 0233 0281 f[1,13] 33 Maj. The shorter reading cannot be discounted as Alexandrian trimming because the scribes of א and B did not shorten the same expression in any of the five other occurrences in Matthew (see 4:25; 8:1; 13:2; 15:30; 19:2). Rather, these verses formed a horizon of expectation for the scribes who added οχλοι in this verse.

12:46–48 | (addition of a verse in bold)

[46] While he was still speaking to the crowds, behold, his mother and brothers stood outside seeking to speak to him. [47] **And someone said to him, "behold, your mother and brothers are standing out side seeking to speak with you.** [48] And he answered the one speaking and said, "Who is my mother and who are my brothers?"

Verse 47 is not present in the earliest MSS (א* B), as well as L Γ and some Old Latin, Syriac, and Coptic MSS. This verse is present in א[(1),] 2 [seventh century] C (D) W Z 33 Maj (so TR and KJV) some Syriac MSS and Coptic MSS. The arguments in favor of its inclusion are twofold: (1) the verse was omitted due to homoeoteleuton (both 12:46 and 12:47 end with the same word, λαλεσαι); (2) Jesus' response in 12:48 requires a response to someone's statement. If 12:47 were missing, Jesus wouldn't be answering anyone. The arguments for the omission are twofold: (1) The array of witnesses supporting the omission is substantial, calling into question whether homoeoteleuton could have occurred in so many witnesses. (2) Scribes would have been prompted by the context to fill in the gap between 12:46 and 12:48, whereas Matthew may have expected readers to do this gap-filling on their own. All things being equal, the text (lacking this verse) has the better support and is the reading which was most likely changed.

13:9, 43 | (added words in bold)

"The one having ears **to hear**, let him hear."

Original Text: ο εχων ωτα ακουετω (**the one having ears, let him hear**). This is the original reading as found in א* B 0242 and other MSS.

Textual Gap-filling: The word ακουειν (to hear) was added in later MSS (א² C D W Z f¹,¹³ 33 Maj) by scribes who wanted to fill out the sense.

13:35 | (added word in bold)
Thus fulfilled the word through **Isaiah [or, Asaph]** the prophet.

Original Text: δια του προφητου (**through the prophet**). This is the original wording according to א¹ B C D L W 0233 0242 Maj.
Textual Gap-filling: Scribes added one of two names here, "Isaiah" or "Asaph." The reading is "through Isaiah the prophet" in א* 33 MSS^according to Eusebius and Jerome; and another is "Asaph the prophet" in MSS^according to Jerome. This textual problem hinges on the fact that Asaph, not Isaiah, was the prophet Matthew quoted. This problem was discussed as early as the third century. Eusebius said that some copyists must not have understood that "the prophet" meant by Matthew was Asaph, and therefore added in the gospel "through Isaiah the prophet," but in the accurate copies it stands without the addition. Thus, Eusebius was arguing for the reading of the text, declaring that it was in the accurate copies. Jerome conjectured that "Asaph was the original reading, for it was found in all the old MSS, but then was removed by ignorant men and replaced with Isaiah." However, not one extant manuscript reads "Asaph." What is interesting, though, is that Jerome was responding to Porphyry (a third-century critic of Christianity) who used this verse to show that Matthew was ignorant. Thus, we know that in the third century some MSS must have read "Isaiah." In defense of the text, it could be said that "Isaiah" was inserted because it was typical for Matthew to name "Isaiah" in prophetic quotations (3:3; 4:14; 8:17; 12:17). In the end, this is clearly a case of scribal gap-filling—scribes attempting to give the prophet a name.

14:30 | (added word in bold)
But when he saw the **strong** wind, he became afraid.

Original Text: τον ανεμον (**the wind**). The original wording is "the wind" as found in א B* 073 33.

Textual Gap-filling: The word ισχυρον (strong) was added in B[1] C D L (W adds "very") 0106 $f^{1,13}$ Maj. It is possible that ισχυρον (strong) was accidentally dropped due to homoeoteleuton—the two previous words both end with the same last two letters. But it is more likely that the adjective was added to intensify the description of the wind. The story compelled scribes to intensify the narrative by making the wind "a strong wind." This addition is in the TR and KJV.

16:2–4 | (addition of verses in bold)

He answered them, "**When it is evening, you say, 'It will be fair weather, for the sky is red.' And in the morning, 'It will be stormy today, for the sky is red and threatening.' You know how to interpret the appearance of the sky, but you cannot interpret the signs of the times.** An evil and adulterous generation seeks a sign. And no sign will be given to it except the sign of Jonah.' And he left them."

These verses in their original, shortened form (lacking 16:2b–3) should read, "He answered them, 'An evil and adulterous generation seeks a sign. And no sign will be given to it except the sign of Jonah.' And he left them." The short text is supported by the earliest MSS (א B) and by X 1424[mg] MSS[according to Jerome] Origen syr cop. Later MSS (C D L W 33 Maj) add, "When it is evening, you say, 'It will be fair weather, for the sky is red.' And in the morning, `It will be stormy today, for the sky is red and threatening.' You know how to interpret the appearance of the sky, but you cannot interpret the signs of the times." Had the additional words been original, there is no good reason to explain why the scribes of א B et al. would have deleted the words on purpose, and there is no way to explain the omission as a transcriptional accident. Thus, it is far more likely and even probable that this portion was not written by Matthew, but inserted later by a scribe who either borrowed the concept from Luke 12:54–56 as a metaphor for "the signs of the times" or inserted these words from an oral or other written tradition to provide an actual example of what it meant for the ancients to interpret the appearance of the sky. Among the added words, there are several that are never used by Matthew or (in two instances) by any other writer in the NT: (1) ευδια = "fair weather" (appears only here in the NT), (2) πυρραζει = "is fiery red" (appears only here in the NT and was used only by Byzantine writers; see BAGD, 731), (3) στυγναζων = "being overcast" (appears only here and in Mark 10:22). This strongly suggests that a scribe added the text. This is, therefore, an eminent example of scribal gap-filling. The addition is in the TR and KJV.

But the question remains: why was this addition made? A close look at the context supplies the answer. According to Matthew's account, the Jewish leaders came to Jesus twice, each time asking him to give them a sign that he was truly the Messiah sent from God. In Matt 12:38, the leaders simply asked for a sign. In response, Jesus said that no sign would be given them but the sign of Jonah, who depicted Christ's death, burial, and resurrection (12:39–40). Later, the Jewish leaders asked Jesus for a sign "from heaven" (Matt 16:1). Again, Jesus told them that no sign would be given them except the sign of Jonah (16:4), according to the reading of the shorter version. But the query for "a sign from heaven" does not seem to be answered by Jesus pointing to Jonah. This created a disappointment for various readers—a gap in the text that called for some kind of filling. Therefore, some scribe decided to fill the gap and did so by borrowing from the thought of Luke 12:54–56 and some other unknown source (perhaps the scribe's own knowledge). He added words about signs in the "sky" as complementing a request about a sign from "heaven."

Whoever filled the gap in Matthew must have done so by the middle of the fourth century, because we know that around 380 Jerome saw MSS with and without the extra words. In fact, Jerome indicated that the extra words were not present in most of the MSS known to him. Nonetheless, he included them in his Latin translation. (The scribe of 1424 noted in the margin of the manuscript that many MSS did not contain these words.) Nearly all English translators have done exactly what Jerome and the scribe of 1424 did: they included the words in the text, knowing there is some doubt about their authenticity.

17:19–21 | (addition of verse in bold)

[19] Then his disciples came to him privately and asked, "Why couldn't we cast it out?" [20] And he said to them, "Because of your little faith. For

truly I tell you if you have faith the size of a mustard seed, you will say to this mountain, 'move from here to there,' and it will move. And nothing will be impossible to you. **[21] But this kind does not come out except by prayer and fasting."**

The earliest MSS (ℵ* B) and 0281 33 it[e] syr[c,s] cop[sa,bo] do not include verse 21, which reads, "but this kind does not come out except by prayer and fasting." This added verse is found in ℵ[2] [seventh century] C D L W $f^{1,13}$ Maj. The evidence against including this verse is substantial, including ℵ* B (the two earliest MSS), 0281 (a seventh-century MS discovered at St. Catherine's Monastery in the late twentieth century), and early witnesses of Old Latin, Coptic, and Syriac. If the verse was originally part of Matthew's gospel, there is no good reason to explain why it was dropped from so many early and diverse witnesses. Thus, it is far more likely that this added verse was assimilated from Mark 9:29 in its long form, which has the additional words "and fasting." In fact, the same MSS (ℵ[2] [seventh century] C D L W $f^{1,13}$ Maj) that have the long form in Mark 9:29 have the additional verse here. Thus, some scribe took the full verse of Mark 9:29 as presented in his manuscript and inserted it here. In short, this is a case where Mark formed the horizon of expectation for Matthew and a scribe filled in the gap accordingly. This addition is in the KJV and TR.

18:10–12 | (addition of verse in bold)
[10] "Take care that you do not despise one of these little ones, for I tell you that in heaven their angels continually see the face of my Father. [11] **For the Son of Man came to save the lost.** [12] What do you think? If a shepherd has a hundred sheep and one wanders off, will he not leave the ninety-nine on the hillside and seek the one that wandered off?

The earliest MSS (ℵ B) do not include 18:11, so also L* $f^{1,13}$ 33 it[e] syr[s] cop[sa] Origen. Several later MSS (D L[c] W 078[vid] Maj syr[c,p]; so TR and KJV) add verse 11 as follows: "For the Son of Man came to save the lost." Still other MSS (L[mg] it[c] syr[h]) expand it as: "For the Son of Man came to seek and to save the lost." The absence of this verse in several important and diverse witnesses attests to the fact that it was not part of the original text of Matthew. It may have been borrowed from Luke 19:10, a passage not at all parallel to this one. Most likely the addition first appeared in the shorter form (variant 1), and was later expanded to the longer form (variant 2), which concurs exactly with Luke 19:10. The MS L demonstrates all three phases: L* omits the verse; L^c has the shorter form of the addition; and L^mg has the longer form.

Very likely this verse was inserted in Matt 18 to provide some sort of bridge between verses 10 and 12. In other words, a scribe perceived there was a semantic gap that needed filling. Luke 19:10 was used to introduce the illustration of a shepherd seeking out its lost sheep (the longer form also speaks of "seeking out," which makes the connection even clearer). However, the text must be read without the bridge 18:11 provides. Verse 12 follows verse 10 in the original in that it provides yet another reason why the "little ones who believe in Jesus" should not be despised: The shepherd is concerned for each and every sheep in the flock. In a flock of one hundred sheep, if even one leaves, he will seek it out and find it.

18:15
If your brother sins **against you**.

Original Text: αμαρτηση (**sins**). This is the original wording according to the two earliest MSS (א B), as well as 0281 f^1 cop^sa Origen.
Textual Gap-filling: The words εις σε (against you) were added. The wording "sins against you" in found in later MSS (D L W 073 f^{13} 33 Maj, so TR and KJV). The earliest testimony supports the shorter text (note the witness of Origen). Furthermore, there is no adequate explanation, on transcriptional grounds, to explain why the words εις σε (against you) would have been omitted from MSS such as א B 0281. The expanded reading is a scribal expansion influenced by 18:21.

19:20 | (added words in bold)
I have kept all things **from my youth**.

Original Text: ταυτα παντα εφυλαξα (**I have kept all these things**). This is the original wording according to early testimony (א* B), as well as L f^1.

Textual Gap-filling: The words εκ νεοτητος μου were added, making the reading, "I have kept all these things from my youth" (ℵ[2] [seventh century] C (D) W *f*[13] 33 Maj; so TR and KJV). The variant reading, a scribal gap-filler, was informed by Mark 10:19 and Luke 18:21—these gospels forming a horizon of expectation for the reading of Matthew, where the words were added.

19:29 | (added words in bold)

Whoever has left houses or brothers or sisters or father or mother **or wife** or children or fields for my sake will receive a hundred times as much and will inherit eternal life.

Original Text: πατερα η μητερα (**father or mother**). This is likely the original wording according to B D it[a].

Textual Gap-filling: Several MSS add η γυναικα (or wife) to the list (ℵ C L W *f*[13] 33), which reads in full "brothers or sisters or mother or father or children or fields." The inclusion could be the result of harmonization to Luke 18:29—Luke forming the horizon of expectation for the reading of Matthew.

20:16 | (added words in bold)

So the last will be first, and the first last, **for many will be called but few are chosen.**

Original Text: The verse ends with "the last will be first and the first, last" according to early and excellent documentary support (ℵ B L Z 085).

Textual Gap-filling: An addition to this is πολλοι γαρ εισιν κλητοι, ολιγοι δε εκλεκτοι (for many are called but few are chosen), as found in C D W *f*[1,13] 33 Maj (so TR and KJV). The gap-filler came from Matthew 22:14. But whereas the statement perfectly suits the conclusion to the parable of the wedding feast in Matthew 22:1–14 (where several are invited but only a few attend), it is an odd addendum to the parable here. Exegetes who use the inferior text will have a difficult time explaining how the statement "many are called but few are chosen" has anything to do with a parable in which all were called and chosen to work in the vineyard. The point of this parable is captured by the shorter, superior original text: "the last will be first and the first, last" because this cancels human endeavor to outdo others and exalts God's sovereignty to give grace as he pleases.

20:22 | (added words in bold)
Jesus answered, "You don't know what you are asking. Are you able to drink the cup I am about to drink **or be baptized with the baptism that I am to be baptized with?"**

Original Text: δυνασθε πιειν το ποτηριον ο εγω μελλω πινειν; (**Are you able to drink the cup that I am about to drink?**) The original text ends here according to early and excellent documentary support: ℵ B D L Z 085 $f^{1,13}$ syr^{c,s} cop^{sa}.
Textual Gap-filling: Other MSS (C W 33 Maj syr^h; so TR and KJV) add "or to be baptized with the baptism that I am baptized with?" The variant reading is a scribal gap-filler borrowed verbatim from Mark 10:38–39—the Gospel of Mark forming a horizon of expectation for reading Matthew. The MSS C and W are notorious for scribal harmonization of the Synoptic Gospels; the majority of MSS (Maj) followed suit.

20:30 | (added word in bold)
Lord **Jesus,** Son of David, have mercy on us.

Original Text: Κυριε . . . υιος Δαυειδ (**Lord, Son of David**). Several early MSS ($\mathfrak{P}^{45vid}$ B C W Z) have the wording, "Lord, Son of David" whether before or after the expression "have mercy on us."
Textual Gap-filling: A few MSS (ℵ L Θ f^{13}) add "Jesus" after "Lord," the result of Mark 10:47 and Luke 18:38 (parallel verses which have the word "Jesus"), forming a horizon of expectation for a scribe that filled the gap accordingly.

21:12 | (added words in bold)
Jesus entered the temple **of God.**

Original Text: το ιερον (**the temple**). The original wording is probably "temple" according to early and good testimony (ℵ B L 0281^vid *f*^13 33).

Textual Gap-filling: This was expanded to "temple of God" in C D W *f*^1 Maj. It is possible that scribes added "of God" when they realized the close connection between this verse and Mal 3:1ff., which predicts that the Messiah would suddenly come to God's temple and purge it. Furthermore, on the basis of documentary support, it must be judged that the variant is a scribal expansion, which happens to give good effect in that the expression "God's temple" stands in strong contrast to the temple profaned with men's merchandising.

21:42–45 | (additional verse in bold)

[42] Jesus said to them, Have you never read the Scriptures, 'The stone the builders rejected has become the cornerstone; this was the Lord's doing and it is amazing in our eyes.' [43] For this reason I say to you that the kingdom of God will be taken away from you [the Jews] and given to a people who will produce its fruit. [44] **The one who falls on this stone will be broken to pieces; and it will crush anyone on whom it falls."** [45] And when the chief priests and the Pharisees heard the parables, they realized he was speaking about them.

The earliest MS ($\mathfrak{P}^{104}$, dated early second century or even c. 100) and other witnesses (D 33 it syr^s Origen Eusebius) do not include 21:44. Other MSS (ℵ B C L W Z 0102 *f*^1,13 Maj syr^c,h,p cop; so TR and KJV) add verse 44: "The one who falls on this stone will be broken to pieces; and it will crush anyone on whom it falls." The inclusion has good documentary support, the kind that would usually affirm legitimacy for most textual variants. However, this is challenged by the earliest manuscript, $\mathfrak{P}^{104}$, as well as Origen, D, and other witnesses. The testimony of $\mathfrak{P}^{104}$ heightens the suspicion that this verse may be scribal gap-filling influenced by Luke 20:18.

The first quote, in Matt 21:42, is taken from Psalm 118:22–23; it is quoted in all the Gospels to underscore the reality that Jesus, though rejected by the Jews, would become the cornerstone of the church. The next verse affirms this truth when it says, "the kingdom of God will be taken away from you [the Jews] and given to a people who will produce its fruit." Then follows 21:44: "he who falls on this stone will be broken to pieces, but he on whom it falls will be crushed" (taken from Isa 8:14–15 and Dan 2:34–35, 44–45). This prophecy depicts Christ as both the stone over which the Jews stumbled and were broken (cf. Rom 9:30–33; 1 Cor 1:23) and the stone that will smash all kingdoms in the process of establishing God's kingdom. The verse doesn't fit in this context at all—a context that has to do with Christ being rejected, not Christ reigning. It is clearly a case of scribal gap filling where a scribe wanted to implicate the Jewish leaders for stumbling over Christ, the stone.

23:13–15 | (additional verse in bold)
[13] "What miseries await you, hypocritical scribes and Pharisees! For you lock people out of the kingdom of heaven. For you do not go in yourselves, and when others are going in, you stop them. [14] **What miseries await you hypocritical scribes and Pharisees! For you devour widows' houses and for the sake of appearance you make long prayers; therefore, you will receive the greater condemnation.** [15] What miseries await you, hypocritical scribes and Pharisees! For you cross sea and land to make a single convert, and you make the convert twice the son of gehenna as you."

Verse 14 is not part of the original text of Matthew according to excellent documentary evidence: ℵ B D L Z f^1 33 it^{a,e} syr^s cop^{sa}. Other MSS (W 0102 0107 f^{13} Maj; so TR and KJV) add here (or after verse 12) verse 14: "What miseries await you hypocritical scribes and Pharisees! For you devour widows' houses and for the sake of appearance you make long prayers; therefore you will receive the greater condemnation." This verse, not present in the earliest MSS and several other witnesses, was taken from Mark 12:40 or Luke 20:47 and inserted in later MSS either before or after 23:13. This is another example where the other gospels formed a horizon of expectation for reading Matthew, and a scribe seeing a gap filled it in accordingly.

24:7 | (added words in bold)
There will be famines, earthquakes, **and pestilences** in various places.

Original Text: λιμοι και σεισμοι (**famines and earthquakes**). The original wording is "famines and earthquakes," according to ℵ B D.

Textual Gap-filling: Other manuscripts add λοιμοι (pestilences), yielding the rendering "famines and pestilences and earthquakes"— in C L W 33 $f^{1,13}$ Maj (so TR and KJV). It is possible that λοιμοι (pestilences) was accidentally dropped from the text because it looks so similar to λιμοι (famines), but it is more likely that λομοι was added to make this verse harmonize with a parallel passage, Luke 21:11. If so, the Gospel of Luke formed the horizon of expectation for the reading in Matthew, and a scribe filled the gap accordingly.

25:1 | (added words in bold)

Ten virgins took their lamps and went out to meet the bridegroom **and the bride.**

Original Text: του νυμφιου (**the bridegroom**). The original wording is "bridegroom" according to excellent testimony (ℵ B C L W Z f^{13}).

Textual Gap-filling: Other MSS add και της νυμφης, yielding the reading, "the bridegroom and the bride" (D Θ f^1 it syr). In a parable about Jesus coming as the bridegroom, many readers would expect that the one who is waiting for him is the bride. This expectation is heightened by the fact that the NT speaks of Christ and the church as bridegroom and bride (John 3:29; 2 Cor 11:2; Eph 5:25–32; Rev 21:2). But for the sake of emphasizing individual readiness for the day of his coming, Jesus used ten bridesmaids, not one bride, to illustrate the importance of being ready. According to custom, on the evening of the wedding the bridegroom would go to the bride's house and take her to his home for the wedding festivities. Along the way, a procession of family and friends would follow the bridegroom and the bride, lighting up the way with their torches. In this parable we see ten bridesmaids who evidently would accompany the bridegroom back to the bride's home; five sensible bridesmaids took enough oil to keep their torches burning, while the other five did not. There is no mention of the bride because this would distract from the lesson of the parable: a call to individual readiness. The scribes and ancient translators (mainly of a "Western" tradition) who added "and the bride" did so (1) to get every character in the scene (according to the historical custom) and/or (2) to reflect the NT theme of Christ, the bridegroom, coming for the church, his bride. Either way, it is a case of scribal gap-filling.

26:3 | (added words in bold)

The leading priests **and scribes [or, Pharisees]** and elders of the people met together.

Original Text: οι αρχιερεις και οι πρεσβυτεροι του λαου (**the leading priests and the elders of the people**). This is the original wording according to the earliest MSS ($\mathfrak{P}^{45}$ ℵ A B) and D L 0293 $f^{1,13}$. **Textual Gap-filling:** Other MSS add γραμματευς or φαρισαιος (scribes or Pharisees), as in the wording "the leading priests and the scribes and the elders" (Maj it; so TR and KJV); and "the leading priests and the Pharisees" (W). According to the best MSS in Matthew, two groups of people were responsible for plotting Jesus' death: the leading priests and the elders of the people, who were the leading members of the Jewish religion and Jewish society. These men are identified by Matthew as the prime movers behind Jesus' murder (26:14; 27:1; 28:12). Along with them, Matthew mentions "the scribes" (26:57; 27:41) and "the Pharisees" (27:62), each of which were added here by various scribes. Thus, this is a case of scribal gap filling, wherein other texts formed a horizon of expectation for their reading of Matt 26:3.

26:28a | (added word in bold)

my blood of the **new** covenant.

Original Text: το αιμα μου της διαθηκης (**my blood of the covenant**). The original wording reads "my blood of the covenant" according to early and diverse testimony: $\mathfrak{P}^{37}$ $\mathfrak{P}^{45vid}$ ℵ L Z Θ 0298vid 33. The original reading has excellent documentation—the four earliest Greek MSS attesting to the reading "covenant." (According to spacing, $\mathfrak{P}^{45}$ could not have contained the word *kaine* = new; see Comfort & Barrett, *Text of Earliest NT Greek MSS*, 164.)

Textual Gap-filling: The wording was changed to "my blood of the new covenant" in A C (D) W $f^{1,13}$ Maj it syr cop by adding καινη (new). Influenced by Luke 22:20, which contains the word "new" before "covenant," later scribes harmonized the Matthean account to Luke's (see note on Luke 22:20). Of course, Jesus was instituting a new covenant, even "the new covenant" God promised through Jeremiah (31:31–34). So, it is not wrong to call this the new covenant, but it is not what Matthew wrote. This is an example where the text in Luke formed a horizon of expectation for Matthew, and a scribe (or scribes) changed Matthew accordingly. The addition is in the TR and KJV.

26:28b
At the end of this verse some late MSS ($C^{3mg\ [ninth\ century]}\ f^{13}$) and lectionaries (124 230 348 543 713 788 826 828 983) add Luke 22:43–44 (in the MSS) or Luke 22:43–45a (in the lectionaries). (For further discussion, see note on Luke 22:43–44.) The earliest witness to the inclusion of this pericope in Matthew 26 is a marginal gloss written by the third corrector of C, who lived in Constantinople in the ninth century. The pericope fits as well in the garden scene in Matthew as it does in Luke, but it is a spurious addition in both books. Its placement in Matthew shows that it was very likely a piece of floating oral tradition. The same kind of multiple placement occured with the pericope of the adulteress (see comments on John 7:53–8:11).

27:16–17 | (added word in bold)
a prisoner named **Jesus** Barabbas

Original Text: Βαραββαν (**Barabbas**). The name of the prisoner is "Barabbas" according to early and diverse testimony: ℵ A B D L W 064 0250 f^{13} 33.
Textual Gap-filling: The name is Ιησους Βαραββαν (Jesus Barabbas) in $S^{mg}\ f^1$ 1 118 579 700 1582 syr^{p,s} MSS$^{according\ to\ Origen}$. The variant reading is supported only by some so-called "Caesarean" witnesses. Some scholars, however, think that "Jesus" was in the archetype of B because the article *ton* was left before *Barraban* (in 27:17), presupposing that the

name "Jesus" appeared before "Barabbas" in the scribe's exemplar. Several later MSS have glosses that indicate "Jesus" appeared in earlier MSS. In a marginal note to codex S (from the tenth century) a certain scribe says, "In many ancient copies which I have met with I found Barabbas himself likewise called 'Jesus.'" According to Metzger, "about twenty minuscules contain a marginal note stating that in very ancient MSS Barabbas is called Jesus; in one of these the note is attributed to Origen. Since Origen himself calls attention to this in his *Commentary on Matthew*, the reading must be of great antiquity." Another argument that has been posited in favor of the reading "Jesus Barabbas" is that it is offset with the wording "Jesus, the one called Christ"—as if the second title serves to distinguish the two men called Jesus (see note in NET). However, this argument is weakened by the fact that Pilate uses the exact same designation a few verses later ("Jesus who is called Christ," 27:22)—as a way of identifying Jesus per his messianic claims, not by way of distinguishing him from another Jesus called Barabbas.

If the reading "Jesus Barabbas" is ancient, why does it not appear in the most ancient MSS (namely, ℵ A B D W)? Was it supressed in most MSS, only to show up later, in ninth- to twelfth-century witnesses? Or was it added by some scribe early in the history of the transmission of the text because he considered "Barabbas" to not really be a name (it means "son of a father") or because he wanted to add some drama to Matthew's narrative? Perhaps the crowd outside Pilate's palace had been shouting, "give us Jesus, give us Jesus." To which Pilate responded, "Do you want Jesus the one called Barabbas or do you want Jesus the one called Christ?" Instead of asking for Jesus the Christ, they get Jesus the murderer. The irony is blatant: The murdering Jesus is set free, while the freeing Jesus is murdered. In the end, I think adding "Jesus" to Barabbas' name is an inventive case of scribal gap-filling.

27:24 | (**added word in bold**)
I am innocent of this man's **righteous** blood.

Original Text: αθωος ειμι απο του αιματος τουτου (**I am innocent of this man's blood**). This is the expression in the earliest MS (B) and D.

Textual Gap-filling: Some MSS add του δικαιου (righteous) to the description of the man, Jesus—namely, ℵ A L W ƒ[1,13] Maj (so TR and KJV). These words are likely a scribal interpolation adapted from Pilate's wife's comment about Jesus being a just man (27:19; cf. Luke 23:14 and John 19:6). This bit of gap-filling is important for the narrative of Jesus' trial because it tells us that Pilate thought Jesus was innocent of the crimes charged against him and even moreso that Jesus was a just man. But as the text reads, it must be inferred that Pilate thought Jesus was innocent or he would not have washed his hands of Jesus' blood.

27:35 | (added words in bold)

When they had crucified him, they divided his clothes by throwing dice, **that it might be fulfilled what was spoken through the prophet, "they parted my garments among them, and for my clothing they threw dice."**

Original Text: διεμερισαντο τα ιματια αυτου βαλλοντες κληρον **(they divided his garments by casting lots)**. This is a quote from Psalm 22:18. The verse ends here according to early and diverse testimony (ℵ A B D L W 33).

Textual Gap-filling: Other MSS (Θ 0250 ƒ[1,13]) add "that it might be fulfilled what was spoken through the prophet, 'they parted my garments among them, and for my clothing they cast lots.'" Because of the excellent support for the shorter text, it must be judged that the long addition was influenced by John 19:24, coupled with a typical Matthean introduction to a prophetic citation (see 4:14). It was natural for scribes, wanting to emulate Matthew's style, to make this addition because Matthew had a penchant for showing how various events in Jesus' life and ministry fulfilled the OT Scriptures (in this case, Psalm 22:18, from the most quoted psalm in the NT concerning the crucifixion). Some of the same scribes (Θ 0250 ƒ[1,13]) did this same gap-filling in Mark 15:27.

28:20

The word αμην (amen) was added in A[c] Θ ƒ[13] Maj (so TR and KJV) by way of scribal gap-filling in the interest of oral reading in church.

Chapter Two

The Gospel of Mark

Mark
1:1 | (added words in bold)
The beginning of the gospel of Jesus Christ, **God's Son.**

Original Text: Ιησου χριστου (**Jesus Christ**). This is the original wording according to P. Oxyrhynchus 5073 ℵ* 28 cop[saMS] Origen.
Textual Gap-filling: Some MSS add υιου θεου (Son of God) making it "the beginning of the gospel of Jesus Christ, God's Son"—so ℵ² [seventh century] (followed many English translations). The documentary evidence favors the shorter title, "Jesus Christ." It is supported by the earliest manuscript (P. Oxy. 5073, an amulet from the late third century), as well as ℵ* and Origen. "God's Son" is an expansion on the title. The same kind of expansion occurred in Peter's proclamation of Jesus' identity (see note on 8:29). Scribes had several verses in mind when they made this expansion, which formed their horizon of expectation. They were disappointed that the text said only "Jesus Christ," and therefore added "Son of God."

1:14 | (added words in bold)
Jesus went into Galilee and proclaimed the gospel **of the kingdom** of God.

Original Text: το ευαγγελιον του θεου (**the gospel of God**). This is the original wording, according to the two earliest MSS (ℵ B), as well as L *f*[1,13].

Textual Gap-filling: Some MSS add της βασιλειας creating the rendering "gospel of God's kingdom" (A D W Maj; so KJV). The variant is the result of scribal harmonization either to the immediate context (the next verse speaks of Jesus proclaiming the imminence of the kingdom) or to another gospel (Matt 4:17). Either one formed a horizon of expectation for the scribe's reading of Mark, and the gap was filled accordingly.

1:34 | (added words in bold)
He would not permit the demons to speak because they knew him **to be Christ.**

Original Text: ηδεισαν αυτον (**they knew him**). The original wording, "they knew him," is found in ℵ A 0130 Maj.

Textual Gap-filling: Some MSS added Χριστον or τον Χριστον. MSS B L W f^1 33^{vid} read "they knew him to be Christ," and ℵ^2 [seventh century] C f^{13} read, "they knew him to be the Christ." The expansions in the variant readings are probably the result of scribal conformity to Luke 4:41, a parallel verse. If so, Luke formed a horizon of expectation for reading Mark, and a scribe filled in the gap accordingly. Or a scribe was motivated by the direct context, in that the reader knows that the demons didn't just know Jesus—they knew his *identity* as the Christ.

1:40 | (added words in bold)
A leper came to him **and fell on his knees** and begged, "if you are willing you can make me clean."

Original Text: παρακαλων αυτον (**begging him**). This is the original wording according to the earliest MS (B), as well as D W.

Textual Gap-filling: Some MSS add και γονυπετων αυτον (and kneeling to him)—so in ℵ A L Maj (so TR and KJV). This expansion came about as the result of scribal conformity to Matt 8:12; Luke 5:12, parallel verses. These two other gospels formed a horizon of expectation for the reading of Mark, and so a scribe filled the gap accordingly.

3:15 | (added words in bold)
to proclaim the gospel [or, to heal diseases] and to have authority to exorcise demons

Original Text: εκβαλλειν τα δαιμονια (**to exorcise demons**). This is the original wording according to the two earliest MSS (‫א‬ B), as well as L. **Textual Gap-filling:** Two variants on this are "to proclaim the good message (το ευαγγελιον) and exorcise demons" (D W), and "to heal diseases (θεραπευειν τας νοσους) and exorcise demons" (A C² [sixth century] D W ƒ¹,¹³ 33 Maj; so TR and KJV). The variants are scribal expansions influenced by Matt 10:1. Matthew formed a horizon of expectation for a scribe's reading of Mark, and the scribe filled the gap accordingly.

3:32 | (added words in bold)
your mother and your brothers **and sisters** are looking for you

Original Text: αδελφοι (**brothers**). This is the original wording, as found in ‫א‬ B C L W ƒ¹,¹³ 33 syr. **Textual Gap-filling:** Some MSS (A D) add και αι αδελφαι σου (and your sisters) producing the rendering "your brothers and your sisters." Although it could be argued that the text is the result of scribal harmonization to Matthew 12:47 and Luke 8:20 or that the phrase "and sisters" was accidentally dropped, the shorter reading has, by far, superior documentary support. Disagreeing with the decision of the majority of NU editors (who included "and sisters"), Metzger (TCGNT) wrote: "The shorter text preserved in the Alexandrian and Caesarean text-types should be adopted; the longer reading, perhaps of Western origin, crept into the text through mechanical expansion. From a historical point of view, it is extremely unlikely that Jesus' sisters would have joined in publicly seeking to check him in his ministry. Thus, it is more likely that the longer text is the result of scribal harmonization to the immediate context (3:35)." In other words, the immediate context formed a horizon of expectation, and a scribe filled the gap accordingly.

5:21 | (added words in bold)
Jesus crossed again **in the boat** to the other side.

Original Text: διαπερασαντος του Ιησου παλιν εις το περαν (**Jesus crossed again to the other side**). This is the original wording according to the earliest MS (𝔓⁴⁵ᵛⁱᵈ), as well as D *f*¹ 28 565 700 it syrˢ.
Textual Gap-filling: Some MSS add εν τω πλοιω (in the boat), creating the rendering, "Jesus crossed again in the boat to the other side" (א A B C L 0132 *f*¹³ 33 Maj; so TR and KJV). The addition is a clear case of scribal gap-filling. The scribe as a reader pictured Jesus in a boat making the crossing, and then just added the words accordingly.

6:44 | (added words in bold)
There were five thousand men who had eaten **the bread**.

Original Text: οι φαγοντες (**those who had eaten**). This is the original wording according to two early MSS (𝔓⁴⁵ א), as well as D W Θ *f*¹,¹³.
Textual Gap-filling: A variant reading is "those who had eaten the loaves" (adding τους αρτους)—so A B L 33 Maj (TR and KJV). A scribe pictured the people eating loaves of bread, so he simply added the words, filling in a perceived gap.

6:45 | (added words in bold)
go on ahead **to the other side** to Bethsaida

Original Text: προαγειν προς Βηθσαιδαν (**go on ahead to Bethsaida**). This is the original wording according to the earliest MS (𝔓⁴⁵ᵛⁱᵈ) and W.
Textual Gap-filling: It is expanded to "go on ahead to the other side to Bethsaida" by adding εις το περαν (א A B C D Maj; so TR and KJV). Picturing Bethsaida on the other side of the lake, a scribe simply added "to the other side."

7:4 | (added words in bold)
the washing of cups, pots, kettles, **and dining couches**

Original Text: χαλκιων (**kettles**). This is the original wording according to the three earliest MSS ($\mathfrak{P}^{45vid}$ ℵ B), as well as L.

Textual Gap-filling: Certain MSS add και κλινων (and dining couches) creating the rendering "kettles and dining couches" (A D W Θ $f^{1,13}$ 33 Maj; so TR and KJV). A scribe noticed that not everything was listed that pertained to eating, so he filled the gap by adding "and couches."

7:14–17 | (added words in bold)

[14] Then he called the crowd again and said to them, "Listen to me, all of you, and understand. [15] There is nothing outside a person that by going in can defile, but the things that come out are what defile. [16] **Let anyone with ears to hear listen.**" [17] And when he left the crowd and entered the house, the disciples asked him about the parable.

The earliest MSS ($\mathfrak{P}$45[vid] ℵ B) and L 0274 do not include 7:16. Other MSS (A D W Θ $f^{1,13}$ Maj; so TR and KJV) add verse 16: "Let anyone with ears to hear listen." A line and letter count of $\mathfrak{P}^{45}$ (which averages thirty-seven lines per page) between one extant page (which ends with 7:15) and the next extant page (which begins at 7:25b), shows that the missing text would be filled with 650 letters in fourteen lines (averaging forty-seven letters per line). This factoring does not leave room for 7:16, thereby showing that $\mathfrak{P}^{45}$ very likely did not include the verse. The extra verse was added by scribes, borrowing it directly from 4:23 (see also 4:9) to provide an ending to an otherwise very short pericope, 7:14–15.

8:29 | (added words in bold)

you are the Christ, **the Son of the living God**

Original Text: συ ει ο χριστος (**you are the Christ**). "The Christ" is the original wording, according to the early testimony of A B C D Origen.

Textual Gap-filling: This is expanded in two ways, (1) "the Christ, the Son of God" (adding ο υιος του θεου in ℵ L), and (2) "the Christ, the Son of the living God" (adding ο υιος του θεου του ζωντος in W f^{13} it[b] syr[p]). The second variant presents scribal conformity of

Mark to Matthew's account verbatim; in Matthew 16:18 Peter tells Jesus, "You are the Christ, the Son of the living God." The first variant is not an exact harmonization from any of the other parallel accounts, because in Luke 9:20 it is "the Christ of God" and in John 6:69, "the holy One of God." The short reading, "the Christ," accords with the beginning of the Gospel of Mark where the best manuscript evidence reads, "the beginning of the gospel of Jesus Christ" (see note on 1:1). The additions show that other texts, as well as preconceived notions of who Jesus was, formed a horizon of expectation for scribes who filled the gap accordingly.

9:19 | (added words in bold)
you faithless **and perverse** generation

Original Text: γενεα απιστος (**faithless generation**). This is the original reading according to several early MSS (א A B C D).
Textual Gap-filling: 𝔓[45vid] and W add και διεστραμμενη (and perverse) creating the rendering, "a faithless and perverse generation." The text of Matthew 17:17, a parallel verse, formed a horizon of expectation for this verse in Mark, and the scribes filled the gap accordingly.

9:24 | (added words in bold)
the father cried out **with tears**

Original Text: κραξας ο πατηρ (**the father cried out**). This is the original reading according to several early MSS (𝔓[45] א A* B C* W).
Textual Gap-filling: This was expanded by adding μετα δακρυων (with tears), creating the rendering "cried out with tears" (A[2] C[3] [ninth century] D Θ f[1,13] Maj; so TR and KJV). Some scribe pictured the man crying with tears, and thereby filled the gap in the text accordingly.

9:29 | (added words in bold)
this is exorcised by prayer **and fasting**

Original Text: εξελθειν ει μη εν προσευχη (**this is exorcised by prayer**). This is the original wording according to the two earliest MSS (א* B), as well as 0274 it^k.

Textual Gap-filling: This is expanded by adding και νηστεια (and fasting), creating the rendering, "this is exorcised by prayer and fasting" (as in א² [seventh century] A C D L W Θ Ψ f^1,13 33 Maj; so TR and KJV). The words "and fasting" were probably added by scribes who were influenced by the early church's strong emphasis on fasting. Therefore, this created a horizon of expectation, and the gap was filled accordingly. (See also notes on Matthew 17:21, Acts 10:30, and 1 Corinthians 7:5 for the same kind of addition.) NA²⁷ lists 𝔓^45vid in support of the longer text, but the lacunae in the manuscript doesn't allow for this supposition.

9:43–48 | (added words in bold)

⁴³ If your hand causes you to sin, cut it off. It is better to enter eternal life with only one hand than to go into the unquenchable fires of gehenna with two hands, ⁴⁴ **where the devouring worm never dies and the fire is never quenched.** ⁴⁵ If your foot causes you to sin, cut it off. It is better to enter eternal life with only one foot then to go into the unquenchable fires of gehenna with two feet, ⁴⁶ **where the devouring worm never dies and the fire is never quenched**. ⁴⁷ And if your eye causes you to sin, gouge it out. It is better to enter the kingdom of God with only one eye than to have two eyes and be thrown into gehenna, ⁴⁸ where the devouring worm never dies and the fire is never quenched.

The earliest and best MSS (א B C L W 0274) do not include verses 44 and 46, which have the same wording as in verse 48. Some scribe added these verses, which appears in other MSS (A D Maj; so TR and KJV) as a kind of poetic refrain: "where the devouring worm never dies and the fire is never quenched." A scribe, envisioning this pericope as a kind of poem, filled two gaps, by adding a refrain to each pronouncement (9:43, 9:45).

9:49 | (added words in bold)

everyone will be salted with fire, **even as every sacrifice will be salted with salt**

Original Text: πας γαρ πυρι αλισθησεται (**everyone is salted with fire**). This is the original wording according to the two earliest MSS (א B), as well as L (W) Δ0274 f¹,¹³ syrs.

Textual Gap-filling: There are two other readings: "every sacrifice will be salted with salt" (D it), and "everyone will be salted with fire, even as every sacrifice will be salted with salt" (A C Θ Ψ Maj; so TR and KJV). The difficulty of this verse led to the textual variants. Among the many interpretations of this text, one of the most acceptable proceeds from the assumption that the "everyone" refers to everyone who follows Jesus. The "fire" can then be understood as a trial or test that a Christian must endure in order to be refined and perfected (see Isa 33:14; Mal 3:2; 1 Cor 3:13, 15; 1 Pet 1:7). But it is the expression "salted with fire" that has created the most difficulty. The best explanation of the origin of this image lies in the Jewish practice of salting a sacrifice. The meal offering was roasted first and then sprinkled with salt to symbolize the perfection of the offering (Lev 2:13). Since salt made the grain good to eat, this act indicated, in a figurative way, that the sacrifice was acceptable to God. Jesus may have had this ritual in mind when he said that everyone of his followers would have to be "salted with fire" in order to be made acceptable before God. With this understanding of the passage, one scribe (perhaps the scribe of D was the originator), borrowing from Leviticus 2:13, changed the verse to read, "for every sacrifice will be salted with salt." Other scribes (as in the second variant) simply appended the gloss with a *kai*. Yet in order for this addition to be a helpful gloss, the *kai* must be understood as functioning epexegetically: "for everyone will be salted with fire, even as every sacrifice will be salted with salt."

10:7 | (added words in bold)
a man will part from his father and mother **and will be joined to his wife**

Original Text: καταλειψει ανθρωπος τον πατερα αυτου και την μητερα (**a man will part from his father and mother**). This is the original reading according to the two earliest MSS (א B), as well as Ψ syrs.

Textual Gap-filling: A variant reading adds και προσκολληθησεται προς την γυναικα αυτου (and will be joined to his wife) creating the rendering "a man will part from his father and mother and be joined to his wife" (in A C D L W Maj; so TR and KJV). It is likely that the extra clause was added by scribes to conform Mark to either Matthew 19:5 or Genesis 2:24 (or both). Therefore, these texts formed a horizon of expectation for scribes, and they filled the gap accordingly.

10:24 | (added words in bold)
How difficult it is **for those trusting in wealth** to enter into the kingdom of God.

Original Text: πως δυσκαλον εστιν εις την βασιλειαν του θεου εισελθειν (**how difficult it is to enter into the kingdom of God**). This is the original reading according to early MSS (א B W it^k).
Textual Gap-filling: This is expanded by adding τους πεποιθοτας επι χρημασιν (for those trusting in wealth) creating the rendering "how difficult it is for those trusting in wealth to enter the kingdom of God" (in A C D Θ f^{1,13} Maj; so TR and KJV). The variant reading is a scribal addition intended to clarify that it is those who trust wealth—not just everybody—who would have a difficult time entering the kingdom of God. Thus, this is a natural case of scribal gap-filling.

11:25–26 | (added words in bold)
^{25} But when you pray, first forgive anyone you are holding a grudge against, so that your Father in heaven may forgive your sins, too. ^{26} **But if you do not forgive, neither will your Father in heaven forgive your trespasses.**

The earliest MSS (א B) and L W Δ Ψ syr^s cop^{sa} do not include 11:26. The MSS A (C D) Θ (f^{1,13} 33) Maj add "but if you do not forgive, neither will your Father in heaven forgive your trespasses." Though it could be argued that verse 26 dropped out by a scribal mistake (both 11:25 and 11:26 end with the same three words), the reading of the text has much better documentation than the variant. Thus, it is more likely that verse 26 is a natural scribal gap-filling, influenced by Matthew 6:15, a parallel verse. In this case, Matthew formed a horizon of expectation for the reading of Mark. The additional words are in the TR and KJV.

14:24 | (added word in bold)
this is my blood of the **new** covenant

Original Text: τουτο εστιν το αιμα μου της διαθηκης (**this is my blood of the covenant**). The original wording is "covenant" according to the two earliest MSS (ℵ B), as well as C D^c L it^k.
Textual Gap-filling: The word καινη (new) was added, producing the reading "new covenant" in A f^{1,13} Maj syr (so TR and KJV). The addition of "new" to "covenant" is the result of scribal gap-filling, wherein scribes were influenced by the liturgical texts, Luke 22:20 and 1 Cor 11:25.

14:68 | (added words in bold)
he went into the entryway **and the rooster crowed**

Original Text: εξηλθεν εξω εις το προαυλιον (**he went out into the entryway**). This is the original wording according to the two earliest MSS (ℵ B), as well as L W Ψ* it^c syr^s cop^{bo}.
Textual Gap-filling: The words και αλεκτωρ εφωνησεν (and the rooster crowed) were added. This scribal gap-filling produces the rendering, "he went out into the entryway and the rooster crowed" in A C D Θ Ψ^c 067 f^{1,13} Maj (so TR and KJV). The documentary evidence strongly supports the shorter reading. Scribes added "and the rooster crowed" because they wanted to emphasize the literal fulfillment of Jesus' prediction in 14:30 and/or because they wanted to account for a first rooster-crowing, because a second one is mentioned in 14:72.

15:27–28 | (added words in bold)
²⁷ Two revolutionaries were crucified with him, one of his right and one on his left. ²⁸ **And the Scripture was fulfilled that said, "He was counted among those who were rebels."**

The earliest and best MSS (ℵ A B C) and D Ψ it^k syr^s cop^{sa} do not include 15:28. L Θ 083 0250 f^{1,13} Maj syr^{h,p} add verse 28. The documentary evidence decisively shows that this verse was not present in any Greek MS prior to the late sixth century (namely, 083—a MS discovered in the 1970s at St. Catherine's Monastery). Influenced by a parallel passage, Luke 22:37 (which is a quotation of Isaiah 53:12), later scribes inserted this verse as a prophetic prooftext for the phenomenon that Jesus died with the lawless. Thus, Luke formed a horizon of expectation for the reading of Mark, and scribes filled in the gap accordingly. The addition is in the TR and KJV.

16:3

One Old Latin manuscript, codex Bobiensis (it[k]), dated c. 400, has an extended gap-filler at the end of this verse: "Suddenly, at the third hour of the day, there was darkness over the whole earth, and angels descended from heaven, and rising in the splendor of the living God they ascended with him [i.e., Jesus], and immediately it was light." This variant, which bears some resemblance to the Gospel according to Peter (35–44), is noteworthy because it is the only attempt to describe the actual resurrection of Jesus. None of the Gospels provide such a description; the reader is simply told that Jesus arose and then the reader (in the other gospels) is given glimpses of Jesus' resurrection appearances. This variant is also significant in that it is found in one of the few MSS that conclude with the shorter ending after 16:8; thus, it is possible that the scribe of it[k], sensing a gap in the text, provided his own resolution to the gospel by including a description of the resurrection in 16:3.

16:8

The Gospel of Mark ends in five ways in various MSS:

1. The earliest MSS (ℵ B) stop at verse 8. This is also evident in 304 syr[s] cop[saMS] arm geo[MSS] Hesychius Eusebius' Canons MSS[according to Eusebius] MSS[according to Jerome] MSS[according to Severus].

2. One MS, codex Bobiensis (it[k]), dated c. 400, supplies a shorter ending, as follows:

And all that had been commanded them they told briefly to those with Peter. And afterward Jesus himself sent out through them, from the east and as far as the west, the holy and imperishable proclamation of eternal salvation. Amen.

3. Other witnesses (A C D Θ f[13] 33 Maj MSS[according to Eusebius] MSS[according to Jerome] MSS[according to Severus] Irenaeus, Apostolic Constitutions, Epiphanius, Severian, Nestorius, Ambrose, Augustine) supply a longer ending:

[9] Now after he rose early on the first day of the week, he appeared first to Mary Magdalene, from whom he had cast out seven demons. [10] She went out and told those who had been with him, while they were mourning and weeping. [11] But when they heard that he was alive and had been seen by her, they would not believe it. [12] After this he appeared in another form to two of them, as they were walking into the country. [13] And they went back and told the rest, but they did not believe them. [14] Later he appeared to the eleven themselves as they were sitting at the table; and he upbraided them for their lack of faith and stubbornness, because they had not believed those who saw him after he had risen. [15] And he said to them, "Go into all the world and proclaim the good news to the whole creation. [16] He who believes and is baptized will be saved; but the one who does not believe will be condemned. [17] And these signs will accompany those who believe: by using my Name they will cast out demons; they will speak in new tongues; [18] they will pick up snakes in their hands, and if they drink any deadly thing, it will not hurt them; they will lay their hands on the sick, and they will recover." [19] So then the Lord Jesus, after he had spoken to them, was taken up into heaven and sat down at the right hand of God. [20] And they went out and proclaimed the good news everywhere, while the Lord worked with them and confirmed the message by the signs that accompanied it.

4. Some MSS (W MSS[according to Jerome]) have this longer ending with an addition after 16:14, which reads as follows:

And they excused themselves, saying, "This age of lawlessness and unbelief is under Satan, who does not allow the truth and power of God to prevail over the unclean things of the spirits. Therefore reveal your righteousness now"—thus they spoke to Christ. And Christ replied to them, "The term of years of Satan's power has been fulfilled, but other terrible things draw near. And for those who have sinned I was handed over to death, that they may return to the truth and sin no more, that they may inherit the spiritual and imperishable glory of righteousness that is in heaven."

5. Some MSS (L Ψ 083 099 274[mg] 579 syr[hmg] cop[sa,boMSS]) have the shorter ending (listed as #2) and the longer ending (listed as #3).

From the outset, I must say that this is one of the clearest examples of scribal gap-filling in the New Testament. Reading a gospel that concluded with 16:8 prompted several scribal attempts at filling a perceived gap. But before I say more on this, let's examine the readings.

The textual evidence for the first reading (stopping at verse 8) is the best. This reading is attested to by ℵ and B (the two earliest extant MSS that preserve this portion of Mark), some early versions (Syriac, Coptic, Armenian, Georgian). Of the church fathers, Clement, Origen, Cyprian, and Cyril of Jerusalem show no knowledge of any verses beyond 16:8. Eusebius, Jerome, and Severus knew MSS that concluded with 16:8. Eusebius said that the accurate copies of Mark ended with verse 8, adding that 16:9–20 were missing from almost all MSS (*Quaestiones ad Marinum* 1—MPG 22, 937). The pericope is also absent from the Eusebian canons. Jerome affirmed the same by saying that almost all the Greek codices did not have 16:9–20 (*Epistle* 120.3 *ad Hedibiam*). Several minuscule MSS (1, 20, 22, 137, 138, 1110, 1215, 1216, 1217, 1221, 1582) that include 16:9–20 have scholia (marginal notes) indicating that the more ancient MSS do not include this section.

Other MSS mark off the longer reading with obeli to indicate its questionable status. The textual evidence, therefore, shows that Mark's gospel circulated in many ancient copies with an ending at verse 8. But this ending seemed to be too abrupt for many readers—both ancient and modern! As a result, various endings were appended. One short ending was appended to round off verse 8 and to indicate that the women had followed the angels' orders in bringing the report to Peter and the disciples. But in order to make this addition, it is necessary to delete the words "and said nothing to no one" from verse 8—which is exactly what was done in it[k].

The most well-known ending is the longer, traditional ending of 16:9–20. The earliest witnesses to this ending come from Irenaeus (via a Latin translation). The other patristic witnesses cited above are no earlier than the fourth century (MSS[according to Eusebius] MSS[according to Jerome] MSS[according to Severus] Apostolic Constitutions [Epiphanius] Severian Nestorius Ambrose Augustine). Thus, we know that this ending was probably in circulation in the third century. It became the most popular of the endings after the fourth century, and was copied again and again in many uncial MSS. Eventually, it was accepted as canonical by the Council of Trent.

But the longer ending is stylistically incongruous with 16:1–8. Any fair-minded reader can detect the non-Markan flavor of the style, tone, and vocabulary of 16:9–20. This is apparent in the very first word in 16:9. The Greek verb *anastas* ("having risen") is an active aorist participle; it conveys the thought that Jesus himself rose from the dead. But almost everywhere else in the Gospels, the passive verb is used with respect to Jesus' resurrection. Furthermore, the additions are all narratively noncontiguous. This is especially apparent in the connection between verses 8 and 9. The subject of verse 8 is the women, whereas the presumed subject of verse 9 is Jesus. And Mary Magdalene is introduced as if she had not been mentioned before or among the women of 15:47–16:8.

This longer ending was made even longer in codex W (the Freer Gospel) with an addition after 16:14. Prior to the discovery of W, we had the record from Jerome that there was another similar ending: "In certain exemplars and especially in the Greek MSS [of the Gospel] according to Mark, at the end of his Gospel, there is written, 'Afterward, when the Eleven reclined at meal, Jesus appeared to them and upbraided them for their unbelief and hardness of heart because they had not believed those who had seen him after his resurrection. And they made excuse, saying, "This age of iniquity and unbelief is under Satan who, through unclean spirits, does not permit the true power of God to be apprehended. Therefore, reveal your righteousness now.'"

The Freer text is an expansion of what was known to Jerome inasmuch as Jesus gives a response to their excuse concerning unbelief. The disciples, blaming Satan for the unbelief, made an appeal to Jesus for his Parousia, which brings the full revelation of his vindictive righteousness. In response, Jesus declares that Satan's time has already come to its end, but before he (Jesus) can reveal his righteous kingdom, there will be a time "of terrible things." This terrible time—of apostasy and judgment—would be the prelude to the second coming.

Finally, some MSS include both the shorter reading and the traditional longer reading. The earliest evidence for these is in two eighth-century MSS, L and Ψ. Some ancient versions (syr[hmg] cop[sa,boMSS]) also have both endings. This is clearly the result of scribal ambiguity—the same kind that is manifest in several modern English versions that print both endings in the text.

What then do we make of the evidence? Scholarly consensus is that Mark did not write any of the endings (2–5 above); all are the work of other hands. Farmer's (*The Last Twelve Verses of Mark*) attempt to defend the view that Mark 16:9–20 was originally part of Mark's gospel, which was later deleted by Alexandrian scribes, is not convincing. Farmer argues that Alexandrian scribes were troubled by the references to picking up snakes and drinking poison and therefore deleted the passage. If they had been troubled by these references, they would have deleted only those verses, not the entire passage! No one else has made a good case for the originality of any of the various additions. The historical fact appears to be that various readers, bothered that Mark ended so abruptly, completed the gospel with a variety of additions. According to Aland ("Bemerkungen zum Schluss des Markusevangeliums," *Neotestamentica et Semitica* [1969], 157–180), the shorter and longer endings were composed independently in different geographical locations, and both were probably circulating in the second century. Metzger says that the longer ending displays some vocabulary (particularly *anisthmi* for *egeiro*) which "suggests that the composition of the ending is appropriately located at the end of the first century or in the middle of the second century" (*Text of the New Testament*, 297).

The reason the shorter ending was created has already been explained. The longer ending was composed afresh or taken verbatim from some other source so as to fill up what was perceived to be a gap in the text of Mark. This writer provided an extended conclusion derived from various sources, including the other gospels and Acts, inserting his own theological peculiarities. The reason the longer ending has become so popular is that it is a collage of events found in the other gospels and the book of Acts. In other words, the other gospels formed a horizon of expectation for the reading of Mark, and scribes filled in the gap accordingly.

Jesus' appearance to Mary Magdalene (16:9) was adapted from John 20:11–17. Her report to the disciples (16:10) was taken from Luke 24:10 and John 20:18. However, the writer of the longer ending has this report concerning Jesus' appearance, whereas Mary's report in John comes after she has seen the empty tomb. John's account is affirmed by the account in Luke 24:11. In both John and Luke the disciples do not believe the report concerning the angelic appearance and the empty tomb; there was no mention yet of any appearance made by Jesus. The change of story in the longer ending to Mark was contrived because Mark 16:8 says that the women said nothing to anybody after seeing the empty tomb and the angelic messenger. The writer couldn't controvert this blatantly (by saying that Mary and/or any of the other women then went to the disciples and told them about the empty tomb), so the writer has Jesus appearing to Mary Magdalene, then Mary telling the disciples, who don't believe. Since this particular account contradicts the authentic gospels, it should be dismissed.

After this, the writer of the longer ending relates Jesus' appearance to two disciples as they were walking from Jerusalem into the country (16:12); this clearly was taken from Luke 24:13–35. The report of further unbelief (16:13) was the interpretation of the composer; Luke does not tell us that the report of the two disciples was disbelieved. Jesus' first resurrection appearance to the disciples (16:14) was borrowed from Luke 24:36–49—with an added emphasis on their unbelief (perhaps adapted from Matthew 28:16–20). Jesus' Great Commission (16:15–16) is loosely based on Matthew 28:19–20—with an emphasis on baptism as a prerequisite to salvation. The promise of signs accompanying the believers (16:17–18) comes from the record of what happened in Acts—including the speaking in tongues (2:4; 10:46) and protection against snakes (28:3–6). The ascension (16:19) is adapted from Luke 24:50–53, and the final verse (16:20) seems to be a summary of the book of Acts, which seems to be preemptively out of place for inclusion in a gospel and is another indication of its spuriousness. (None of the other gospels tell us anything about the disciples' work after Jesus' resurrection and ascension.)

Even though much of this longer ending was drawn from other gospels and Acts, the composer had an unusual emphasis on the disciples' unbelief in the resurrection of Christ. In this regard, the composer may have been following through on the Markan theme of identifying the unbelief and stubbornness of the disciples. Indeed, this gospel, more than any other, focuses on the disciples' repeated failures to believe Jesus and follow him. The composer of the longer ending also had a preference for belief and baptism as a requisite for salvation, as well as an exalted view of signs. Christians need to be warned against using this text for Christian doctrine because it is not on the same par as verifiable New Testament Scripture. Nothing in it should be used to establish Christian doctrine or practice. Unfortunately, certain churches have used Mark 16:16 to affirm dogmatically that one must believe and be baptized in order to be saved, and other churches have used Mark 16:18 to promote the practice of snake-handling. (Even some boxes that keep the rattlesnakes are marked with "Mark 16:18" written on them.) Those who are bitten by rattlesnakes, they believe, will not be harmed if they are true followers of Christ. The writer of the longer ending also emphasized what we would call charismatic experiences—speaking in tongues, performing healings, protection from snakes and poison. Although the book of Acts affirms these experiences for certain believers, they are not necessarily the norm for all.

The longer ending of W (noted also by Jerome) was probably a marginal gloss written in the third century that found its way into the text of some MSS prior to the fourth century. This gloss was likely created by a scribe who wanted to provide a reason for the unbelief that is prevalent in the longer ending. Satan is blamed for the faithlessness, and an appeal is made for Jesus to reveal his righteousness immediately. But this revelation would be postponed until after a time of terrible things. This interpolation may have been drawn from several sources, including Acts 1:6–7; 3:19–21; and the Epistle of Barnabas 4:9; 15:7. In any case, it is quite clear that Mark did not write it. The style is blatantly non-Markan.

Having concluded that Mark did not write any of the endings, we are still left with the question: Did Mark originally conclude his gospel with verse 8, or was an original extended ending lost?

In defense of the view that Mark originally ended his gospel at verse 8, four arguments can be posited: (1) As is, the gospel ends with an announcement of Christ's resurrection. Jesus doesn't need to actually appear in resurrection to validate the announcement. Our demand that the gospel must record this appearance comes from our knowledge of the other gospels. Mark did not have to end his gospel the way the others did. (2) Mark, as a creative writer, may have purposely ended abruptly in order to force his readers to fill in the gap with their own imaginations. Perhaps Mark did not want to describe—or think himself capable of describing—the resurrection of Christ and/or the risen Christ; thus, he left it to the readers to imagine how the risen Christ appeared to Peter and the other disciples. (3) Throughout this gospel, Mark presented a secrecy motif concerning Jesus being the Messiah (see note on 8:26). The final verse is the culmination of this motif: The women "said nothing to anyone." Of course, the reader knows that this silence would not last; indeed, the very opposite will happen—the word of Christ's resurrection will be announced to the disciples, and the disciples will proclaim this to the world. Thus, the ending was calculated by Mark to be the irony of ironies; perhaps he thought it would bring a smile to the face of the Christians reading or hearing this gospel for the first time, for they knew how the word had gone out! (4) It ends on a note of failure—the women's failure to go to Peter and the other disciples—because this is consistent with another major theme in Mark's gospel: discipleship failure. All these four reasons could account for Mark purposely concluding the gospel at 16:8.

Many readers are not satisfied with these reasons—primarily because they, having read the other gospels, have a different horizon of expectation for the conclusion of Mark. Thus, many readers have questioned whether it was Mark's original design to conclude with verse 8. Why conclude with merely an announcement of Jesus' resurrection and a description of the women's fear and bewilderment? In the Gospel of Mark, a pattern is set in which every one of Jesus' predictions is actually fulfilled in narrative form. According to Gundry (*Mark: A Commentary on His Apology for the Cross*, 1009), the predictions that were fulfilled were as follows: God's kingdom having come with power at the transfiguration, the finding of a colt, the disciples' being met by a man carrying a jar of water, the showing of the upper room, the betrayal of Jesus by one of the Twelve, the scattering of the rest of the Twelve, the denials of Jesus by Peter, the Passion, and the Resurrection. Thus, since Jesus announced that he would see his disciples in Galilee (14:28), the narrative should have depicted an actual appearance of the risen Christ to his disciples in Galilee.

Since there isn't such a record (even in the additions), some readers have thought that an original extended ending got lost in the early transmission of Mark's gospel—probably because it was written on the last leaf of a papyrus codex and was torn away from the rest of the manuscript. (Though Mark may have originally been written on a scroll, which would have preserved the last section rolled up inside, copies of Mark in codex form would have been in use as early as the end of the first century; see Comfort, *Encountering the Manuscripts*, 27–40). This codex could have contained just the Gospel of Mark or all four gospels set in the typical Western order: Matthew, John, Luke, Mark (which was likely the case for $\mathfrak{P}^{45}$). In both scenarios, Mark 16 would have been the last sheet. However, it seems very odd and most unusual that this ending would not have survived in some MS somewhere. The history of textual transmission is characterized by tenacity; once a reading enters the textual stream, it will usually be preserved in some MS and show up somewhere down the line. Thus, this imagined ending to Mark must have been lost very soon after the composition of the gospel, if there was such an ending.

It is possible that 16:7 was intended to be the concluding verse of the first paragraph of the Mark's original last chapter (inasmuch as it concludes with the glorious angelic announcement of Christ's resurrection) and that 16:8 was the first sentence of the next paragraph. It seems that the last two words of 16:8, *ephobounto gar* ("for they were afraid"), could have been the first two words of a new sentence. Indeed, it is highly unusual for a sentence, let alone an entire gospel, to end with the conjunctive *gar*; so it is likely that some word or words followed, such as *ephobounto gar lalein* ("for they were afraid to speak . . . "). After this, Mark's narrative would have continued to relate, most likely, that Jesus appeared to the women (as in Matthew and John), and that the women, no longer afraid, then went and told the disciples what they saw. This would have probably been followed by Jesus appearing to his disciples in Jerusalem and in Galilee. This is the basic pattern found in the other gospels. And since Mark was probably used by the other gospel writers, it stands to reason that their narrative pattern reflects Mark's original work.

16:20

The word αμην (amen) was added in C* D L W Θ f^{13} Maj (so TR and KJV) by way of scribal gap-filling, wherein the word was added in the interest of oral reading in church.

Chapter Three

The Gospel of Luke

Luke
1:28 | (added words in bold)
The Lord is with you. **Blessed are you among women.**

Original Text: ο κυριος μετα σου (**the Lord is with you**). This is the original wording according to three early MSS (**א** B W), as well as L.
Textual Gap-filling: Other MSS (A C D Θ $f^{1,13}$ Maj; so TR and KJV) add ευλογημενη συ εν γυναιξιν (blessed are you among women). The variant reading is an expansion borrowed from 1:42, where it is Elizabeth who says that Mary is "blessed among women." This shows that Luke 1:42 formed a horizon of expectation for Luke 1:28, and a scribe filled the gap accordingly.

4:4 | (added words in bold)
man does not live by bread alone **but by every word of God**

Original Text: ουκ επ αρτω μονω ζησεται ο ανθρωπος (**man does not live by bread alone**). This is the original wording according to the two earliest MSS (**א** B), as well as L W syr^s cop^{sa}.
Textual Gap-filling: A variant reading adds αλλα παντι ρηματι θεου (but by every word of God) creating the rendering, "man does not live by bread alone but by every word of God" in A (D) Θ Ψ (0102) $f^{1,13}$ 33

Maj (so KJV). This shows scribal gap-filling, wherein Matthew formed a horizon of expectation for a scribe's reading of Luke, and he filled the gap accordingly, bringing Luke in conformity with Matthew 4:4, a parallel verse. The OT quotation comes from Deuteronomy 8:3.

4:5 | (added words in bold)
the devil led him up **a high mountain**

Original Text: αναγαγων αυτον (**he led him up**). This is the original wording according to the two earliest MSS (ℵ* B) and L.
Textual Gap-filling: The text is filled by adding εις ορος υψηλον, creating the rendering "the devil led him up a high mountain." This occurs in ℵ² [seventh century] A D W 0102 33 Maj (so TR and KJV). Matthew 4:8, a parallel verse, formed the horizon of expectation for the reading of Luke, and a scribe (or scribes) filled in the gap accordingly.

4:8 (added words in bold)
Jesus answered, "**Get behind me, Satan.**"

Original Text: αποκριθεις ο Ιησους (**Jesus answered**). This is the original wording according to the two earliest MSS (ℵ B) and D L W f¹.
Textual Gap-filling: The words υπαγε οπισω μου σατανα were added, creating the rendering, "Jesus answered him, 'Get behind me, Satan.'" This is the reading in A Θ Ψ 0102 f¹³ Maj (so TR and KJV). Matthew 4:10, a parallel verse, formed the horizon of expectation for the reading of Luke, and a scribe (or scribes) filled in the gap accordingly.

4:18 | (added words in bold)
He has sent me **to heal the broken-hearted**, to proclaim release to the captives.

Original Text: απεσταλκεν με (**he has sent me**). There is strong testimony for this reading (ℵ B D L W).
Textual Gap-filling: To this was added ιασασθαι τους συντετριμμενους την καρδιαν (to heal the broken-hearted) in

A Θ Ψ 0102 Maj (so TR and KJV). Scribes added the phrase to make it conform to Isaiah 61:1–2, the Scripture quoted here. In this case, Isaiah formed the horizon of expectation for the reading of Luke, and the gap was filled accordingly.

4:41 | (added words in bold)
you are **the Christ,** the Son of God

Original Text: ο υιος του θεου (**the Son of God**). This is the original wording according to early and excellent testimony ($\mathfrak{P}^{75}$ ℵ B C D L W). $\mathfrak{P}^{75}$ is not listed in NA[27], but it supports the text (see Comfort & Barrett, *Text of Earliest NT Greek MSS*, 508).
Textual Gap-filling: ο χριστος (the Christ) is added, creating the rendering, "you are the Christ, the Son of God" in A Q Θ 0102 $f^{1,13}$ Maj. The variant is a scribal expansion, a bit of gap-filling, that occurred in almost every Gospel text where Jesus is identified by others as "the Son of God."

5:38 | (added words in bold)
New wine is poured into fresh wineskins **so that can be preserved.**

Original Text: οινον νεον εις ασκους καινους βλητεον (**new wine is poured into fresh wineskins**). This is the original wording according to early and excellent testimony ($\mathfrak{P}^4$ $\mathfrak{P}^{75vid}$ ℵ B L W).
Textual Gap-filling: και αμφοτεροι συντηρουνται (and both are preserved) was added, creating the rendering, "new wine is poured into fresh wineskins so that both can be preserved" in A C (D) Θ Ψ Maj (so TR and KJV), by way of scribal conformity to Matthew 9:17, a parallel verse. The text of Matthew formed a horizon of expectation for the reading of Luke, and the gap was filled in accordingly.

6:1 | (added words in bold)
he went through a grainfield on **the second-first** sabbath

Original Text: εν σαββατω (**on a sabbath**). This is the original reading according to early and excellent testimony ($\mathfrak{P}^4$ $\mathfrak{P}^{75vid}$ ℵ B L W f^1 33).

Textual Gap-filling: The word δευτεροπρωτω (second first) was added creating the rendering, "the second first Sabbath" in A C D Θ Ψ Maj, a scribal gap-filler. Westcott and Hort (*The New Testament in the Original Greek: Introduction and Appendix*, 58) suggest that some copyist added *proto* (first) as a correlative to the "other Sabbath" mentioned in 6:5, which was then changed to *deutero* (second) by another scribe in light of 4:31. Both words were retained and combined in subsequent copies.

7:10 | (added words in bold)
found the servant, **who had been sick,** healed

Original Text: ευρον τον δουλον υγιαινοντα (**found the servant healed**). This is the original wording according to four early MSS (𝔓[75] ℵ B W), as well as *f*[1] it cop.
Textual Gap-filling: A variant reading adds ασθενουντα (who had been sick), creating the rendering, "found the servant, who had been sick, healed." This is scribal gap-filling found in A C (D) Θ Ψ *f*[13] 33 Maj (so TR and KJV).

7:39 | (added word in bold)
if he were **the** prophet, he would know what kind of woman was touching him

Original Text: προφητης (**prophet**). 𝔓[75vid] ℵ A B[2] D L W Θ Ψ *f*[1,13] 33 Maj. The Pharisees said, "if he were a prophet, he would know what kind of woman was touching him." 𝔓[75] is not listed in NA[27], but it supports the text (see Comfort & Barrett, *Text of Earliest NT Greek MSS*, 508).
Textual Gap-filling: Two MSS (B* Ξ) prefix a definite article before προφετες (prophet) thereby creating the reading, "the Prophet." As happened elsewhere in the NT text (see note on John 7:52), such an addition was intended to show that Jesus was "the Prophet" like Moses (Deut 18:15; Acts 3:22–23; 7:37).

8:25 | (added words in bold)
he commands even the winds and water **and they obey him**

Original Text: τοις ανεμοις επιτασσει και τω ωδατι (**he commands even the winds and the water.**) This is the original wording according to the two earliest MSS ($\mathfrak{P}^{75}$ B).

Textual Gap-filling: All other MSS add και υπακουουσιν αυτω (and they obey him), creating the rendering, "he commands even the winds and the water, and they obey him," by way of scribal conformity to Matthew 8:27, a parallel verse. In this case, Matthew formed a horizon of expectation, and the gap was filled accordingly. The addition is found in the TR and KJV.

8:43 | (added words in bold)

though she had spent all she had on physicians, she could not get anyone to cure her

Original Text: ουκ ισχυσεν απ ουδενος θεραπευθηναι (**she could not get anyone to cure her**). This is the original wording according to $\mathfrak{P}^{75}$ B (D) 0279 syr^s cop^{sa} Origen. The earliest MSS ($\mathfrak{P}^{75}$ B), plus 0279 (discovered in the 1970s at St. Catherine's Monastery), affirm the shorter text.

Textual Gap-filling: An expanded reading adds ιατρος προς αναλωσασα ολον τον βιον creating the reading, "though she had spent all she had on physicians, she could not get anyone to cure her" (in ℵ A C L W Θ Ξ Ψ $f^{1,13}$ 33 Maj; so TR and KJV). The longer text was influenced by Mark 5:26, a parallel verse. So the text of Mark formed a horizon of expectation for the reading of Luke, and the gap was filled accordingly.

8:45 | (added words in bold)

Peter **and those with him** said, "Master, the crowds are surrounding you and pressing against you."

Original Text: ο πετρος (**Peter**). The original wording is "Peter" according to the two earliest MSS ($\mathfrak{P}^{75}$ B), as well as syr cop.

Textual Gap-filling: Other MSS add και οι συν αυτω (and those with him) creating the rendering, "Peter and those who were with him" in

א A C³ [ninth century] D L W Θ Ξ Ψ f^{1,13} 33, by way of scribal conformity to Mark 5:31, a parallel verse. Thus, Mark formed a horizon of expectation for the reading of Luke and the gap was filled accordingly.

9:35 | (added words in bold)
This is my son, the chosen One, **my beloved in whom I am well pleased.**

Original Text: ο υιος μου ο εκλελεγμενος (**my Son, the chosen One**). This is the original wording according to early and excellent testimony (𝔓⁴⁵ 𝔓⁷⁵ א B itᵃ syrˢ cop).

Textual Gap-filling: Two variant readings add αγαπητος "my beloved" (A C* W f^{13} 33 Maj) and αγαπητος εν ω ηυδοκησα "my beloved in whom I am well pleased" (C³ [ninth century] D Ψ). As often happened in the textual transmission of the Gospels, divine proclamations about Jesus were harmonized. At Jesus' transfiguration, each of the Synoptic Gospels has different wording. Matthew 17:5 reads, "this is my beloved Son, in whom I am well pleased"; Mark 9:7 reads, "this is my beloved Son"; and Luke 9:35 reads, "this is the Son, the chosen One." The first variant is a harmonization to Mark, and the second to Matthew (or perhaps Luke 3:22). The reading of the texts, supported by the four earliest MSS (𝔓⁴⁵ 𝔓⁷⁵ א B), is without question the one Luke wrote. The wording in Luke reveals the twofold position of Jesus as both God's Son and the chosen One—that is, the Father chose his Son to be the Messiah. Luke's wording is reminiscent of Psalm 2:7 and especially Isaiah 42:1 (LXX), which speaks of the messianic Servant. This chosen Servant was destined to carry out God's will by suffering death on the cross. This entirely suits the context which speaks of Jesus' "exodus from Jerusalem" (9:31).

9:54 | (added words in bold)
command fire to come down from heaven and consume them, **as also Elijah did**

Original Text: ειπωμεν πυρ καταβηναι απο του ουρανου και αναλωσαι αυτους (**command fire to come down from heaven and**

consume them). This is the original wording according to early and excellent testimony ($\mathfrak{P}^{45}$ $\mathfrak{P}^{75}$ ℵ B L).

Textual Gap-filling: This is expanded by adding ωϛ και Ηλιαϛ εποιησεν (as also Elijah did) creating the rendering, "command fire to come down from heaven and consume them, as also Elijah did" in A C D W Θ Ψ $f^{1,13}$ 33 Maj (so TR and KJV), influenced by 2 Kings 1:10. In this case 2 Kings formed the horizon of expectation for the reading of Luke, and the gap was filled accordingly.

9:55–57 | (added words in bold)

55 "But he turned and rebuked them, **and said, "You do not know what spirit you belong to. 56 For the Son of Man has not come to destroy human lives but to save them."** 57 And they went to another village.

The original wording does not include the words in bold, according to early and excellent testimony ($\mathfrak{P}^{45}$ $\mathfrak{P}^{75}$ ℵ A B C L W). This was expanded in D (for the first sentence only) K Γ Θ $f^{1,13}$ it syr. The original wording says only that Jesus rebuked them; the actual words of the rebuke are not recorded. Dissatisfied with this gap in the narrative, scribes provided two additions—a short one (in D) and a longer one (perhaps built on the other). Most likely, the longer addition (found in the TR and KJV) was influenced by Luke 19:10.

11:2a | (added words in bold)
our Father **in the heavens**

Original Text: Πατερ (**Father**).
This is the original wording according to $\mathfrak{P}^{45vid}$ $\mathfrak{P}^{75}$ ℵ B syr^s.

Textual Gap-filling: This is expanded by adding ημων ο εν τοιϛ ουρανοιϛ creating the rendering "our Father in the heavens" in A C W Θ Ψ 070 f^{13} 33^{vid} Maj it syr^{c,h,p} cop (so TR and KJV) by way of scribal conformity to Matthew 6:9, a parallel verse. The text of Matthew formed the horizon of expectation for the reading of Luke, and the gap was filled accordingly.

11:2b | (added words in bold)
May your kingdom come. **May your will be done on earth as it is in heaven.**

Original Text: ελθετω η βασιλεια σου (**may your kingdom come**). This is the original wording according to early and excellent testimony: 𝔓⁷⁵ ℵ A B C L W *f*¹·¹³ 33 itᵃ·ᵇ·ᶜ·ᵉ syr cop.

Textual Gap-filling: There are two variant readings: one adds εφ ημας (upon us) creating the rendering, "may your kingdom come upon us" (D itᵈ), and another reads ελθετω το πνευμα σου το αγιον εφ ημας και καθαρισατω ημας ("may your Holy Spirit come upon us and cleanse us") in 700. Other MSS (ℵ A C D W *f*¹³ 33ᵛⁱᵈ Maj it syrʰ·ᵖ copᵇᵒ; so TR and KJV) add γενηθητω το θελημα σου ως εν ουρανω και επι της γης ("let your will be done on earth as it is in heaven") by way of scribal conformity to Matthew 6:10, a parallel verse. In this case, the text in Matthew formed the horizon of expectation for the reading of Luke, and the gap was filled accordingly.

11:4 | (added words in bold)
Don't lead us into temptation, **but rescue us from evil.**

Original Text: μη εισενεγκης ημας εις πειρασμον (**don't lead us into temptation**). This is the original wording according to the three earliest MSS (𝔓⁷⁵ ℵ*·² B), as well as L syrˢ copˢᵃ.

Textual Gap-filling: Other MSS (ℵ¹ A C D W Θ Ψ 070 *f*¹³ 33 Maj it syrᶜ·ʰ·ᵖ) add αλλα ρυσαι ημας απο του πονηρου (but rescue us from evil) by way of scribal conformity to Matthew 6:13, a parallel verse. In this case, the text in Matthew formed the horizon of expectation for the reading of Luke, and the gap was filled. The addition is found in the TR and KJV.

11:25 | (added word in bold)
finds the house **empty,** swept

Original Text: ευρισκει σεσαρωμενον (**it finds it swept**). The original wording is "swept" according to the testimony of two early MSS (𝔓⁷⁵ ℵ*), as well as A D W 070 Maj.

Textual Gap-filling: A textual variant adds σχολαζοντα (empty), creating the reading "empty and swept" in ℵ² [seventh century] B C L *f*¹·¹³ 33, by way of scribal conformity to Matt 12:44, a parallel verse. The text in Matthew formed a horizon of expectation for the reading of Luke, and the gap was filled accordingly.

11:33 | (added words in bold)
after lighting a lamp no one hides it **or puts it under a basket**

Original Text: ουδεις λυχνον αψας εις κρυπτην τιθησιν (**no one, after lighting a lamp, hides it**). This is the original wording according to the two earliest MSS (𝔓⁴⁵ 𝔓⁷⁵), as well as L 070 *f*¹ syrˢ copˢᵃ.
Textual Gap-filling: This is expanded by adding ουδε υπο τον μοδιον, creating the rendering "no one hides it or puts it under a basket" in ℵ A B C D W *f*¹³ Maj (so KJV), by way of scribal conformity to Matthew 5:15 and Mark 4:21, parallel verses. Thus, Matthew and Mark created the horizon of expectation for the reading of Luke, and the gap was filled accordingly.

12:24 | (added words in bold)
consider **the birds of the sky and** the ravens

Original Text: κατανοησατε τους κορακας (**consider the ravens**). This is the original wording according to early and excellent testimony: 𝔓⁷⁵ ℵ A B C D W Maj.
Textual Gap-filling: This is expanded by adding τα πετεινα του ουρανου creating the reading "the birds of the sky and the ravens" in 𝔓⁴⁵, by way of scribal conformity to Matthew 6:26, a parallel verse. Thus, the text of Matthew formed a horizon of expectation for the reading of Luke, and the gap was filled in accordingly.

12:31 | (added words in bold)
the kingdom **of God**

Original Text: την βασιλειαν αυτου (**his kingdom**). This is the original reading in three early MSS (𝔓⁷⁵ ℵ B), as well as D* L Ψ.

Textual Gap-filling: The word θεου (of God) was added, creating the expanded reading "the kingdom of God" in 𝔓⁴⁵ A D¹ Q W Θ 070 f¹,¹³ 33 Maj (so TR and KJV). This was natural gap-filling by scribes who wanted to fill in whose kingdom was being discussed.

12:39 | (added words in bold)
he would have watched and he would have not let his house been broken into

Original Text: ουκ αν αφηκεν διορυχθηναι τον οικον αυτου (**he would not have let his house be broken into**). This is the original wording according to two early MSS (𝔓⁷⁵ ℵ*), as well as (D) it^{e,i} syr^{c,s}.

Textual Gap-filling: This was expanded by adding εγρηγορησεν ("guarded"), creating in rendering "he would have watched and he would have not let his house been broken into" in ℵ¹ (A) B L Q W Θ Ψ 070 f¹,¹³ 33 Maj, by way of scribal conformity to Matthew 24:43, a parallel verse. Thus, Matthew formed the horizon of expectation for the reading of Luke, and the gap was filled accordingly.

13:19 | (added word in bold)
it grew and became **a great tree**

Original Text: δενδρον (**a tree**). This is the original wording according to early and excellent testimony: 𝔓⁷⁵ ℵ B D L 070.

Textual Gap-filling: This was expanded to δενδρον μεγα ("great tree") in 𝔓⁴⁵ A W Θ Ψ 0303 f¹³ 33 Maj (so TR and KJV). Although it could be argued that "great" was deleted by scribes in order to conform this text to Matthew 13:32 (a parallel verse), it is just as likely that the word was added to heighten the sense. Besides, the MSS with the shorter text (especially 𝔓⁷⁵ ℵ B) generally show far less harmonization in the Gospels than those that have the addition.

13:35 | (added word in bold)
your house is left to you **desolate**

Original Text: αφιεται υμιν ο οικος υμων (**your house is left to you**). This is the original wording according to early and excellent testimony: 𝔓⁴⁵ᵛⁱᵈ 𝔓⁷⁵ ℵ A B L W syrˢ copˢᵃ.

Textual Gap-filling: A variant reading adds ερημος, creating the reading "your house is left to you desolate" in D N Δ Θ Ψ ƒ¹³ 33 Maj it syrᶜ (so TR and KJV). Whereas in Matthew 23:38 the best documentation supports the inclusion of the word "desolate," in Luke it is just the opposite. It is quite likely that D et al. added ερημος (desolate) to Luke from their text of Matthew 23:38, so that in these MSS Matthew 23:38 and Luke 13:35 perfectly harmonize. Thus, Matthew formed a horizon of expectation for the reading of Luke, and the gap was filled accordingly.

15:16

Original Text: χορτασθηναι (**wanted to satisfy himself**). This is the original wording according to 𝔓⁷⁵ ℵ B D L ƒ¹,¹³. The three earliest MSS (𝔓⁷⁵ ℵ B) support the text.

Textual Gap-filling: This was changed to γεμισαι την κοιλιαν αυτου ("he wanted to fill his stomach") in A (W) Θ Ψ Maj (so TR and KJV). This gap-filling provides a fuller description of the prodigal son's condition.

15:21 | (added words in bold)

I am no longer worthy to be called your son; **make me as one of your hired servants.**

Original Text: ουκετι ειμι αξιος κληθηναι υιος σου (**I am no longer worthy to be called your son**). This is the original wording according to the earliest MS (𝔓⁷⁵) and A L W Θ Ψ ƒ¹,¹³ Maj syrᶜ,ˢ cop.

Textual Gap-filling: Some MSS add ποιησον με ως ενα των μισθιων σου, creating the expansion "I am no longer worthy to be called your son; make me as one of your hired servants" in ℵ B D 33 syrʰ. There are two factors that favor the reading of the original text: (1) it has earlier and more diverse testimony, and (2) the words in the variant were carried over from Luke 15:19 so that the son's actual speech would replicate the one he had planned. This is natural gap-filling of a narrative.

16:19b–20

This is the only parable told by Jesus in which one of the characters is given a name; the blind beggar is called Lazarus. Some witnesses provide testimony of scribal attempts (beginning as early as the second century) to also give the rich man a name. The scribe of $\mathfrak{P}^{75}$ provided him a name, *Neues*; and one Coptic Sahidic manuscript reads *Nineue*. Both of these names may be synonyms for Nineveh, the wealthy city that came under God's judgment. According to a pseudo-Cyprianic text (third century), the rich man is called "Finaeus." Priscillian also gave him the name "Finees," which is probably an alternate to Phinehas, Elezar's companion (Exod 6:25; Num 25:7, 11). Peter of Riga called him Amonofis, which is a form of "Amenophis," a name held by many Pharaohs (see TCGNT). These namings all exemplify the scribal desire to fill perceived gaps in the narrative text.

17:24 | (added words in bold)

So it will be with the Son of Man **in his day.**

Original Text: ουτως εσται ο υιος του ανθωπου (**so it will be with the Son of Man**). This is the original wording according to the two earliest MSS ($\mathfrak{P}^{75}$ B) and D it cop[sa].

Textual Gap-filling: To this was added εν τη ημερα αυτου (in his day) creating the rendering "so it will be with the Son of Man in his day" (א A L W Θ Ψ $f^{1,13}$ Maj syr cop[bo]; so TR and KJV). Scribes may have added "in his day" to make a parallel statement with 17:22 ("you will desire to see one of the days of the Son of Man"), or scribes could have dropped the phrase to make it conform to the Matthean parallel (Matt 24:47). However, since the scribes of $\mathfrak{P}^{75}$ and B were rarely given to harmonization, it seems more likely that "in his day" was added later as a piece of gap-filling.

17:35–36 | (added text in bold)

[35] There will be two women grinding grain together; one will be taken and the other left. [36] **Two will be in the field; one will be taken and the other left.**

The earliest MSS ($\mathfrak{P}^{75}$ ℵ B) do not include 17:36. This verse, found in later MSS (D f^{13} 700) and versions (it syr) reads, "Two will be in the field; one will be taken and the other left." It is quite likely that the verse is the result of scribal gap-filling influenced by Matthew 24:40, with harmonization to the style of Luke 17:35.

18:24 | added words in bold)
Jesus saw him **become very sad.**

Original Text: ιδων δε αυτον ο Iησους (**Jesus saw him**). This is the original wording according to the two earliest MSS (ℵ B), as well as L f^1 cop. **Textual Gap-filling:** A variant reading adds περιλυπτον γενομενον creating the rendering "Jesus saw him become very sad"—so A (D) W 078 f^{13} Maj syr. The shorter text has better support than the variant, which appears to be scribal filling of the narrative, carried over from 18:23.

21:38
It is interesting to note that the eight MSS belonging to f^{13} (13 69 124 346 543 788 826 983) include the pericope of the adulteress after this verse. The insertion of this story (probably taken from an oral tradition) at this place in Luke's narrative is a much better fit than where it is typically placed in John's narrative (between 7:52 and 8:12). In John, it interrupts the connection between the Sanhedrin's rejection of Jesus (on the basis that he was a Galilean) and Jesus' following rejoinder. Chronologically, the story belongs in Jesus' last week in Jerusalem, at a time when he was going back and forth between the Temple (to teach in the day time) and the garden of Gethsemane (to sleep at night). Thematically, the story belongs with the others that show the religious leaders trying to trap Jesus into some kind of lawlessness and thereby have grounds to arrest him. These encounters, according to the Synoptic Gospels, also appear in Jesus' last days in Jerusalem.

    The group of MSS, f^{13}, could represent the earliest positioning of the pericope of the adulteress, which was then transferred to the end of John 7, or it could represent an independent positioning. Westcott and Hort (*The New Testament in the Original Greek, Introduction and*

Appendix, 63) said this passage was probably known to a scribe "exclusively as a church lesson, recently come into use, and placed by him here on account of the close resemblance between Luke 21:37–38 and John 7:53–8:2. Had he known it as part of a continuous text of St John's Gospel, he was not likely to transpose it." It is also possible that the earliest scribe of a manuscript in the group of *f* ¹³ (either the composer of the archetype in Calabria or the scribes of 124 and/or 788) made the editorial decision to move it from its usual spot at the end of John 7, to follow Luke 21. This transposition, which was a good editorial decision, affirms the transitory nature of the pericope of the adulteress—which is to say, it was not treated on the same par as fixed, inviolable Scripture. (See comments on John 7:53–8:11.)

22:42–45 | (added words in bold)

⁴² Father, if you are willing, take this cup from me; yet not my will but yours be done. ⁴³ **Then an angel from heaven appeared to him and strengthened him.** ⁴⁴ **And in his anguish he prayed more fervently, and his sweat was like drops of blood falling to the ground.** ⁴⁵ When he got up from prayer, he came to the disciples and found them sleeping, exhausted from grief.

Nearly all the most ancient MSS ($\mathfrak{P}^{69\text{vid}}$ $\mathfrak{P}^{75}$ $\aleph^1$ A B T W) do not include 22:43–44. These verses, found in $\aleph^{*,2\ [\text{seventh century}]}$ D L Θ Ψ 0171ⁱᵈ 0233 Maj (so TR KJV) read, "Then an angel from heaven appeared to him and strengthened him. And in anguish he prayed more fervently, and his sweat was like drops of blood falling to the ground." Several other witnesses could be cited for exclusion and inclusion of the verses. Church fathers (Jerome, Hilary) knew of MSS both with and without these verses, several MSS that include the verses (Δᶜ Πᶜ 892ᶜ 1079 1195 1216 copᵇᵒᴹˢˢ) are marked with obeli to signal suspicion about their right to be in the text, and *f* ¹³ places the verses after Matthew 26:39.

The editors of $\mathfrak{P}^{69}$ (see P. Oxyrhynchus 2383), were fairly confident that the only way to account for the size of the lacuna in $\mathfrak{P}^{69}$ (from Luke 22:41 to Luke 22:45) is that the copyist's exemplar did not contain Luke 22:43–44 and that the scribe's eye moved from *proshuceto* in 22:41 to *proseuche* in 22:45. The editors calculated that these two words would have been on the end of lines, four lines apart. The manuscript 0171 should be listed as "vid" (as in UBS[4]) inasmuch as it shows only a portion of 22:44; however, there are no obeli or asterisks as noted in UBS[4]. (For the reconstructions of $\mathfrak{P}^{69}$ and 0171 respectively, see Comfort & Barrett, *Text of Earliest NT Greek MSS*, 471–472, 687–691.)

The manuscript evidence is decidedly in favor of the exclusion of 22:43–44. The Greek MSS (dating from the second to fifth century) favoring the exclusion of these verses forms an impressive list: $\mathfrak{P}^{69vid}$ $\mathfrak{P}^{75}$ $\aleph^1$ B T W. (The first corrector of $\aleph$ was a contemporary of the scribe who produced the manuscript of Luke; indeed, he was the diorthotes who worked on this manuscript before it left the scriptorium.) Other signs of its doubtfulness appear in MSS marking the passage with obeli or crossing out the passage (as was done by the first corrector of $\aleph$). Its transposition to Matthew 26 in some MSS and lectionaries indicates that it was a free-floating passage that could be interjected into any of the passion narratives (see note on Matt 26:39).

The manuscript support for including the verses involves several witnesses, the earliest of which is 0171[vid] (c. 300). None of the other MSS are earlier than the fifth century. However, several early fathers (Justin, Irenaeus, Hippolytus, Dionysius, Eusebius) acknowledged this portion as part of Luke's gospel. When we turn to the writings of other early church fathers, we discover that many noted both the presence and absence of the "bloody sweat" passage in the MSS known to them. We have notes on this from Jerome, Hilary, Anastasius, and Epiphanius. For example, Epiphanius (*Ancoratus* 31.4–5) indicated that the verses were found in some "uncorrected copies" of Luke. This tells us that in the early course of textual transmission, the Gospel of Luke (in this chapter) was being copied in two forms—one that lacked the "bloody sweat" passage and one that included it.

The question, then, is: Did Luke write these verses, which were later deleted, or did someone else add them later? Metzger's view of this is true: "On grounds of transcriptional probability it is less likely that the verses were deleted in several different areas of the church by those who felt that the account of Jesus overwhelmed with human weakness was incompatible with his sharing the divine omnipotence of the Father, than that they were added from an early source" (TCGNT). Westcott and Hort also considered the "bloody sweat" passage to be an early (second century) interpolation, added from an oral tradition concerning the life of Jesus (see Westcott and Hort, *The New Testament in the Original Greek: Introduction and Appendix*, 64–67). I consider the "bloody sweat" passage to be the result of scribal gap-filling. The text reads seamlessly from 22:42 to 22:45, and then is interrupted by 22:43–44.

23:16–18 | (added words in bold)

[16] [Pilate said,] "I will therefore have him flogged and release him." [17] **It was necessary for him to release one prisoner for them at the festival.** [18] But they all shouted out together, "Take this man away! Release Barabbas for us!"

Several early MSS ($\mathfrak{P}^{75}$ A B T), as well as L 070 892[txt] it[a] cop[sa], do not include 23:17. This verse ("it was necessary for him to release one [prisoner] for them at the festival") is included in ℵ W (Θ Ψ) $f^{1,13}$ 892[mg] Maj (D syr[c,s] after 23:19). Since this verse is absent from several significant MSS and is transposed in D and syr[c,s], its presence in the other MSS is most likely the result of scribal interpolation—borrowing primarily from Mark 15:6, as well as Matthew 27:15. The verse was probably added to provide a reason for the crowd's request that Pilate release Barabbas instead of Jesus (23:18). But the text reads contiguously from 23:16 to 23:18, joining Pilate's statement about releasing Jesus to an immediate plea from the crowd to release Barabbas instead. Thus, verse 17 is clearly the result of Matthew and Mark forming the horizon of expectation for the reading of Luke, and the gap was filled in accordingly. The addition is in the TR and KJV.

23:33–34 | (added words in bold)

[33] When they came to the place that is called "the Skull," they crucified him, along with the criminals, one on his right and one on his left. [34] **And Jesus said, "Father, forgive them, for they do not know what they are doing."** Then they threw dice to divide his clothing.

Several early MSS ($\mathfrak{P}^{75}$ $\aleph^1$ B D* W), as well as Q 070 it[a] syr[s] cop[sa], do not include 23:34a. This verse ("And Jesus said, 'Father, forgive them, for they do not know what they are doing'") is included in $\aleph^{*,2}$ [seventh century] (A) C D[2] (E with obeli) L 0250 $f^{1,(13)}$ Maj syr[c,h,p] Diatessaron Hegesippus. The omission of these words in early and diverse MSS (the earliest being $\mathfrak{P}^{75}$) cannot be explained as a scribal blunder. But were the words purposely excised? Westcott and Hort (*The Original Greek New Testament: Introduction and Appendix*, 68) considered willful excision to be absolutely unthinkable. But Marshall (*The Gospel of Luke*, 867–868) can think of several reasons why scribes might have deleted the words—the most convincing of which is that scribes might have been influenced by an anti-Judaic polemic and therefore did not want the text saying that Jesus forgave the Jews who killed him. This would be especially true for codex Beza (D), whose scribe has been charged with having anti-Judaic tendencies (see Epp, *The Theological Tendency of Codex Cantabrigiensis in Acts*). However, there are four MSS—of diverse traditions—earlier than D (namely, $\mathfrak{P}^{75}$ B W it[a]), which do not include these words. Thus, D could not have been responsible for being the first to eliminate the words. The primary argument against excision (on the basis of an anti-Judaic polemic) is that Jesus was forgiving his Roman executioners, not the Jewish leaders. The grammar affirms this; in 23:33 it says *estaurosan auton* ("they [the Roman execution squad] crucified him"), then in 23:34 Jesus says, *aphes autois* ("forgive them")—i.e., the Roman execution squad. Furthermore, Jesus had already pronounced judgment on the Jewish leaders who would not believe in him and even worse who proclaimed that his works were empowered by Beelzebul, the prince of demons (Matt 12:24–32).

It is easier to explain that the words were not written by Luke but were added later (as early as the second century—for it is attested to by Hegesippus and the Diatessaron). If the words came from an oral tradition, many scholars are of the opinion that they are authentic. Indeed, Westcott and Hort (*The New Testament in the Original Greek: Introduction and Appendix*, 67) considered these words and 22:43–44 to be "the most precious among the remains of the evangelic tradition which were rescued from oblivion by the scribes of the second century."

But what if the words did not come from an oral tradition about Jesus' life and sayings? What would have inspired their inclusion? My guess is that the words were added to make Jesus the model for Christian martyrs—of offering forgiveness to one's executioners. Whoever first added the words may have drawn from Acts 7:60, where Stephen forgives his executioners. Since Stephen's final words parallel Jesus' final utterances (cf. Acts 7:56 to Luke 22:69; Acts 7:59 to Luke 23:46), it seemed appropriate to have Luke 23:34 emulate Acts 7:60. Or the words could have come from martyrdom stories, such as the account of the execution of James the Just, who is said to have forgiven his executioners (Eusebius' *Ecclesiastical History* 2.23, 16). Thus, it can be imagined that church leaders told would-be martyrs to forgive their executors because Jesus had done the same. In the end, Luke 23:34a is a prime example of scribal gap-filling. The addition is in the TR and KJV.

23:38 | (added words in bold)
And there was an inscription over him **written in Greek and Latin and Hebrew.**

Original Text: ην δε και επιγραφη επ αυτω (**and there was an inscription over him**). This is the original wording according to several early MSS ($\mathfrak{P}^{75}$ $\aleph^1$ B C*), as well as L 070 cop^{sa} syr^{c,s}.
Textual Gap-filling: To this was added γραμμασιν ελληνικοις και ρωμαικοις και εβραικοις (written in Greek and Latin and Hebrew) in $\aleph^{*,c}$ A C^3 D W 0250 $f^{1,13}$ Maj (so TR and KJV). Borrowing from John 19:20, several scribes added an expression naming the three languages written on the placard nailed to Jesus' cross. This addition doesn't follow John 19:20 exactly, because John's order is Hebrew, Latin, Greek. In any event, scribes were influenced by John as their horizon of expectation, and filled in the gap accordingly.

24:32 | (added words in bold)
Didn't our hearts burn **within us?**

Original Text: ουχι η καρδια ημων καιομενη ην (**Didn't our hearts burn?**) This is the original wording according to the two earliest MSS (𝔓^{75} B), as well as D syr^{c,s}.

Textual Gap-filling: A variant reading adds εν ημιν, creating the reading "didn't our hearts burn within us" (א A L W 33 Maj; so TR and KJV), by way of scribal expansion, filling in the gap.

24:36 | (added words in bold)

And he said to them, 'Peace be with you. **I am [here]; do not be afraid'**"

Original Text: και λεγει αυτοις ειρηνη υμιν (**and he said to them, "Peace be with you."**) This is the original wording according to four early MSS (𝔓^{75} א A B), as well as L cop syr^{c,s}.

Textual Gap-filling: This was expanded by adding εγω ειμε, μη φοβεισθε, creating the rendering, "and he said to them, 'Peace to you. I am [here]; do not be afraid'" in 𝔓 (W) syr^{h,p} cop^{boMSS}. The phrase is omitted in D it. The first variant is a scribal addition borrowed from John 6:20. The statement εγω ειμι (I am) adds a theophanic element to this Christophany. The second variant was considered original by Westcott and Hort (see note above on Luke 24:3), who believed that the longer text was a scribal interpolation borrowed from John 20:19. (WH included the words, though in double brackets.) But Luke and John probably derived their accounts about the resurrection from many of the same sources; thus, this verbal equivalence is not unusual. In the end, the addition was a product of scribal gap-filling.

24:53

Later MSS (A B C^2 [sixth century] Θ Ψ f^{13} Maj; so TR and KJV) add αμην ("amen"). Because the NT books were read orally in church meetings, it became customary to end the reading with an "amen." Gradually, this spoken word was added to the printed page of many late MSS. This gap-filling took place in all four gospels and Acts.

Chapter Four

The Gospel according to John

John
1:36 | (added words in bold)
The lamb of God, **the One taking away the sin of the world.**

Original Text: ο αμνος του θεου (**the Lamb of God**): This is the original reading according to excellent testimony ($\mathfrak{P}^{66c}$ $\mathfrak{P}^{75}$ ℵ B L W T).
Textual Gap-filling: Some MSS ($\mathfrak{P}^{66*}$ C* W) add ο αιρων την αμαρτιαν του κοσμου (the one taking away the sin of the world). This is scribal gap-filling, wherein John 1:29 formed a horizon of expectation for John 1:36, and the perceived gap was filled in accordingly.

3:13 | (added words in bold)
the Son of Man, **the One being in heaven**

Original Text: ο υιος του ανθρωπου (**the Son of Man**). This is the original wording according to $\mathfrak{P}^{66}$ $\mathfrak{P}^{75}$ ℵ B L W^s [seventh century] 083 086 cop Diatessaron. This reading was also known to many church fathers, such as Origen, Didymus, and Jerome.
Textual Gap-filling: This is expanded by adding ο ων εν τω ουρανω creating the rendering "the Son of Man the One being in heaven" in (A*) Θ Ψ 050 $f^{1,13}$ Maj (so TR and KJV). The longer reading appears in some later Greek MSS, was known to many early church fathers

(Hippolytus, Origen, Dionysius, Hesychius, Hilary, Lucifer, Jerome, Augustine), and was translated in some early versions (primarily Old Latin and Syriac). From a documentary perspective, the shorter reading is more trustworthy. So, the longer reading is the result of scribal gap-filling wherein a scribe (or scribes) wanted to make it clear that Jesus (from their perspective) is now heaven.

3:15 | (added words in bold)
the one believing in him **may not perish but** have eternal life

Original Text: ο πιστευων εν αυτω εχη ζωην αιωνιον (**the one believing in him may have eternal life**). This is the original reading according to excellent testimony ($\mathfrak{P}^{36}$ $\mathfrak{P}^{66}$ $\mathfrak{P}^{75}$ ℵ B L T W^s 083 086 f^1 33). **Textual Gap-filling:** Some MSS ($\mathfrak{P}^{63}$ A Θ Ψ f^{13} Maj; so TR and KJV) add μη αποληται αλλα creating the rendering "the one believing in him may not perish but have eternal life." This is scribal gap-filling, creating parallelism with the following verse. This shows that a scribe knew 3:16 before he copied 3:15, and made the change accordingly.

3:31–32 | (added words in bold)
[31] The one who comes from above is superior to all. The one who is from the earth and speaks earthly things. The one who comes from above **is superior to all.** [32] He testifies about what he has seen and heard, but no one accepts his testimony.

The phrase "is superior to all" is omitted in $\mathfrak{P}^{75}$ ℵ* D f^1 it syr^c. It is included in $\mathfrak{P}^{36vid}$ $\mathfrak{P}^{66}$ ℵ^2 A B L W^s [seventh century] Θ Ψ 083 086 33 f^{13} Maj syr^{h,p,s} cop^{bo} (so TR and KJV). The manuscript evidence for both readings is evenly split. The early papyri, $\mathfrak{P}^{66}$ and $\mathfrak{P}^{75}$, are divided, as are ℵ and B, and the ancient Syriac and Coptic versions; thus, they neutralize each other's testimony. Furthermore, good reasons could be given to defend why scribes would be tempted to add the words "is superior to all," as a repeat from the first part of the verse, or delete the words because they seemed redundant. Therefore, this is a case where either reading could be original. But if the words were added, they are the product of scribal gap-filling—carried over from 3:31. With the phrase absent, the text reads "the one who comes from above testifies about what he has seen and heard."

3:34 | (added word in bold)
God gives the immeasurable Spirit.

Original Text: ου γαρ εκ μετρου διδωσιν το πνευμα (**for he gives the immeasurable Spirit**). The earliest MSS ($\mathfrak{P}^{66}$ $\mathfrak{P}^{75}$ $\mathfrak{P}^{80vid}$ ℵ) and B² C* L W^s [seventh century] indicate it is the Son who gives the immeasurable Spirit.
Textual Gap-filling: Other MSS, mainly later (A C² D Maj), supply the subject, ο θεος ("God"), yielding the sense that "God gives the immeasurable Spirit." This is a simple case of scribal gap-filling, but it skews the message. Jesus, not God, is the one who gives the immeasurable Spirit.

4:42 | (added words in bold)
this is the Savior of the world, **the Christ**

Original Text: ο σωτηρ του κοσμου (**the Savior of the world**). This is the original wording according to early, excellent testimony: $\mathfrak{P}^{66}$ $\mathfrak{P}^{75}$ ℵ B C* W^s [seventh century].
Textual Gap-filling: This is expanded by adding ο χριστος creating the wording "this is the Savior of the world, the Christ" in A C³ D L Θ Ψ $f^{1,13}$ 33 Maj (so TR and KJV). This is a case of scribal gap-filling wherein a fuller title of Jesus seemed more appropriate to the context.

5:3–4 | (added words in bold)
³ A great number of sick, blind, blame, and paralyzed people were lying in these walkways, **waiting for a certain movement of the water,** ⁴ **for an angel of the Lord came from time to time and stirred up the water. And the first person to step in after the water was stirred was healed of whatever disease he had.**

The earliest MSS ($\mathfrak{P}^{66}$ $\mathfrak{P}^{75}$ ℵ B) and other MSS (A* C* L T cop) do not include 5:3b–4. Other MSS (A^c C^3 Θ Ψ 078^vid Maj; so TR and KJV) add 5:3b–4. These words were added by later scribes to help explain why the water bubbled up (5:7). Thus, the greater context of John 5:1–9 formed a horizon of expectation for these verses, and the gap was filled in accordingly.

5:44 | (added word in bold)
the glory from the one and only **God**

Original Text: την δοξαν την παρα του Μονου (**the glory from the One and Only**). This reading is supported by the three earliest MSS ($\mathfrak{P}^{66}$ $\mathfrak{P}^{75}$ B) and W^s [seventh century].
Textual Gap-filling: This is expanded by adding θεου (God), creating the rendering "the glory from the one and only God" in $\mathfrak{P}$63^vid ℵ A D L Δ Θ Ψ 0210^vid f^{1,13} 33 Maj it^e syr. The text, which has early documentation, was expanded by adding "God." The title του Μονου is titular in and of itself; it expresses the one who is "the One and Only." Of course, this is God, but "God" doesn't need to be added for the title to make sense.

6:69 | (added words in bold)
the Christ, the Holy One of God
the Christ, the Son of the living God

Original Text: ο αγιος του θεου (**the Holy One of God**). This is the original wording according to most of the earliest MSS ($\mathfrak{P}^{75}$ ℵ B C* D W).
Textual Gap-filling: Two significant variant readings are ο χριστος ο αγιος του θεου ("the Christ, the Holy One of God") in $\mathfrak{P}^{66}$ cop and ο χριστος ο υιος του ζωντος θεου ("the Christ, the Son of the living God") in Θ^c Ψ 0250 f^{13} syr Maj; so TR and KJV). The reading of the text is superior to the other variant readings because of its excellent documentary support and because the other variant readings are obvious assimilations to Matthew 16:16 ("the Christ, the Son of the living God") or some derivation thereof. Thus, Matthew formed a horizon of expectation for the reading of John, and the gap was filled accordingly.

7:39 | (added words in bold)
as yet there was no **Holy** Spirit **given**

Original Text: ουπω γαρ ην πνευμα (**as yet there was no Spirit**). This is the original wording according to four early MSS ($\mathfrak{P}^{66c}$ $\mathfrak{P}^{75}$ ℵ T), as well as Θ Ψ.

Textual Gap-filling: A variant reading is ουπω γαρ ην αγιος πνευμα ("as yet there was no Holy Spirit") in $\mathfrak{P}^{66*}$ L W 0105 $f^{1,13}$ 33 Maj. Another variant is ουπω γαρ ην πνευμα δεδομενον ("the Spirit had not yet been given") in B it[a,aur,b,c] sy[c,s,p]. The verb "given" was added in B and by ancient translators (Old Latin and Syriac) to complete the sense. The idea in the Greek is that the Spirit of Jesus was not available to believers until after Jesus had been glorified through death and resurrection. Both expansions are the result of scribal gap-filling.

7:52–8:12 | (added words in bold)

[52] They replied, "You aren't from Galilee too are you? Search and you will see that no prophet comes from Galilee?" [53] **Each of them went home,** [1] **while Jesus went to the Mount of Olives.** [2] **Early in the morning he came to the temple. When the people came to him, he sat down and began to teach them.** [3] **The scribes and the Pharisees brought a woman who had been caught in adultery. Making her stand before all of them,** [4] **they told him, "Teacher, this woman was caught in the act of committing adultery.** [5] **The law of Moses commands us to stone such women. But what do you say?"** [6] **They were testing him, so as to bring some charge against him. Jesus bent down and with his finger wrote on the ground.** [7] **When they persisted in questioning him, he sat up and said to them, "Let him who is without sin be the first to throw a stone at her."** [8] **Once again he bent down and wrote on the ground.** [9] **When they heard this, they went away, one by one, beginning with the elders. Jesus was left alone with the woman standing before him.** [10] **Jesus sat up and said to her, "Woman, where are they now? Has anyone condemned you?"** [11] **She answered, "No one, Lord." And Jesus replied, "Neither do I condemn you. Go your way, and don't sin again."** [12] Then Jesus spoke

out again, "I am the light of the world. The one who follows me will never walk in darkness, but will have the light of life."

The most ancient Greek MSS and other MSS do not include John 7:53–8:11, namely 𝔓[39vid] 𝔓[66] 𝔓[75] ℵ A[vid] B C[vid] L N T W Δ Θ Ψ 0141 0211 33 565 it[a,f] syr[c,s,p] cop[sa,bo,ach2] geo. Its omission is also attested to by the Diatessaron Origen Chrysostom Cyril Tertullian Cyprian MSS[according to Augustine] MSS[according to Jerome]. The passage is found in later MSS (with various verse lengths) and in different positions in the Gospels: D (F) G H K M U G it[aur,c,d,e] syr[h,pal] cop[boMSS] Maj MSS[according to Didymus] 7:53–8:11; E 8:2–11 with asterisks; L 8:3–11 with asterisks; f[1] after John 21:25; f[13] after Luke 21:38 (see note there); 1333[c] 8:3–11 after Luke 24:53; 225 after John 7:36. The passage, which is clearly a later addition, came from an oral tradition and was included in the TR and KJV. It does not belong in John's gospel as part of the original text. It is the result of scribal gap-filling, scribes adding this piece of oral tradition in various places in the Gospels. (Papias, who knew John, was aware of a story where Jesus saved a woman from death.) The addition in this place in John is because there seems to be no connection between 7:53a and 8:12, but there is. The connection has to do with the Pharisees claiming that the Scriptures say nothing about a prophet arising from Galilee. But they do.

But John 8:12ff. contains Jesus' rebuttal to the Pharisees who had boldly told Nicodemus that the Scriptures make no mention of the prophet (or even a prophet), much less the Christ, being raised up in Galilee (7:52). With respect to this assertion, Jesus made a declaration in which he implied that the Scriptures did speak of the Christ coming from Galilee. He said, "I am the light of the world; he who follows me will not walk in darkness, but will have the light of life." This statement was probably drawn from Isaiah 9:1–2: "But there will be no more gloom for her who was in anguish; in earlier times he treated the land of Zebulun and the land of Naphtali with contempt, but later on he will make it glorious, by the way of the sea, on the other side of the Jordan, Galilee of the Gentiles. The people who walk in darkness will see a great light, and the light will shine on those who live in the shadow of death." Both passages contain parallel images. Both Isaiah 9:2 and John 8:12 speak about the Messiah coming as the light among those who are walking in darkness and sitting under the shadow of death, to give them the light of life.

The story of the woman caught in adultery (who was then saved by Jesus from being stoned to death) is a famous text. Many people quote from the line "Let him who is without sin be the first to throw a stone at her," when trying to emphasize the point that no one has the right to judge others because there are no persons without sin. In other words, I can't condemn anyone for their sin because I also am a sinner. A saying close to this message is: "no one who lives in a glass house should throw stones at others." Only Jesus has the right to condemn but even he doesn't do so. He said, "I have not come into the world to condemn it but to save it" (John 3:17).

9:37–39 | (added words in bold)

[37] Jesus told him, "You have seen him, and he is the One speaking to you. [38] **He said, "Lord, I believe," and he worshiped him.** [39] Jesus said, "For judgment I have come into the world, so that those who do not see may gain their sight, and the ones who see may become blind."

Three early MSS ($\mathfrak{P}^{75}$ ℵ* W) and it[b] cop[ach2,saMSS] do not include 9:38–39a. Other MSS ($\mathfrak{P}^{66}$ ℵ[2] A B D L Δ Θ Ψ Maj; so TR and KJV) add 9:38–39a. Though the manuscript evidence is evenly divided, the additional words probably came from early baptismal liturgy in which the person being baptized confesses, "Lord, I believe." Thus, this is a case of scribal gap-filling wherein scribes were influenced by ecclesiastical tradition. The text without the addition reads seamlessly: "Jesus told him, 'You have seen him and he is the One speaking to you. For judgment I came into the world, so that those who do not see may gain their sight, and the ones who see may become blind.'" (For more on this, see Comfort, *NT Text and Translation Commentary*, 293–294).

10:8 | (added words in bold)

All who came **before me** were thieves and robbers.

Original Text: παντες οσοι ηλθον κλεπται εισιν λησται (**all who came were thieves and robbers**). This is the original wording according to three early MSS ($\mathfrak{P}^{45\text{vid}}$ $\mathfrak{P}^{75}$ ℵ*), as well as Γ Δ Maj it syr$^{\text{p,s}}$ cop.

Textual Gap-filling: A variant reading adds προ εμου (before me) creating the reading, "all who came before me were thieves and robbers" in $\mathfrak{P}^{66}$ ℵ^2 A B D L W Ψ $f^{1,13}$ 33 syr$^{\text{h}**}$. The words "before me" were added to give the statement better sense. But implicit in the words "all who came" is the idea of claiming to be the Messiah-shepherd. Thus, this is a case of scribal gap-filling, wherein scribes thought Jesus' statement needed clarification.

10:26 | (added words in bold)
you are not my sheep, **as I said to you**

Original Text: ουκ εστε εκ των προβατων των εμων (**you are not my sheep**). This is the original wording according to several early MSS ($\mathfrak{P}^{66\text{c}}$ $\mathfrak{P}^{75}$ ℵ B W), as well as L Θ 33.

Textual Gap-filling: A variant reading adds καθως ειπον υμιν creating the rendering, "you are not my sheep, as I said to you" in $\mathfrak{P}^{66*}$ A D Ψ $f^{1,13}$ Maj, by way of scribal expansion.

12:1 | (added words in bold)
Bethany, where Lazarus was, **the one who had died**

Original Text: Βηθανιαν οπου ην Λαζαρος (**Bethany, where Lazarus was**). This is the original wording according to several early MSS ($\mathfrak{P}^{75}$ ℵ B D W).

Textual Gap-filling: Some MSS add ο τεθνηκως ("the one who died"), creating the reading, "in Bethany where Lazarus was, who had died" in $\mathfrak{P}^{66}$ A D Θ Ψ 0217^{vid} 0250 $f^{1,13}$ 33 Maj (so TR and KJV). This is a clear example of scribal gap-filling.

13:31–32 | (added words in bold)
[31] When Judas had gone out, Jesus said, "Now the Son of Man is glorified, and God had been glorified in him. [32] **If God is glorified in him,** God will also glorify him in himself, and he will immediately glorify him.

The original wording does not include the words in bold, according to early and excellent testimony: 𝔓⁶⁶ ℵ* B C* D L W syrˢ·ʰ copᵃᶜʰ. Another reading adds, "If God is glorified in him" in ℵ² A C² Θ Ψ 0233 *f*¹³ Maj it syrᵖ copˢᵃ (so TR and KJV) by way of scribal gap-filling.

16:26 | (added words in bold)
I will ask the Father **concerning you.**

Original Text: εγω ερωτησω τον πατερα (**I will ask the Father**). This is reading in two early MSS (𝔓⁵ᵛⁱᵈ 𝔓⁶⁶).
Textual Gap-filling: Other MSS add περι υμων (concerning you): 𝔓²²ᵛⁱᵈ ℵ A B D W. This is scribal gap-filling to make the sense more understandable.

18:40 | (added words in bold)
They **all** shouted **again.**

Original Text: εκραυγασιν ουν (**they shouted**). This is the reading in the earliest MS (𝔓⁶⁶ᵛⁱᵈ), as well as K N Ψ *f*¹·¹³ 33.
Textual Gap-filling: Another variant reading is "they shouted again" (adding παλιν) in 𝔓⁶⁰ ℵ B L W 0109; another variant (adding παντες) is "they all shouted again" in A (Dˢ) Θ 0250 Maj. The two additions are most likely the product of scribal gap-filling.

19:20
Original Text: γεγραμμενον Εβραιστι, Ρωμαιστι, Ελληνιστι (**written in Hebrew, Latin, and Greek**). This is the original wording according to three early MSS (𝔓⁶⁶ᵛⁱᵈ ℵ¹ B), as well as L N Ψ 33. The text has superior support, including that of 𝔓⁶⁶, whose reading is based on my publication of new fragments of 𝔓⁶⁶ (see Comfort, "New Reconstructions and Identifications of New Testament Papyri," in *Novum Testamentum* XLI [1999], 3:214–230; see p. 229). Prior to my publication, it could not be said that 𝔓⁶⁶ preserved this order, for the first two words were completely missing. 𝔓⁶⁶ now provides the earliest testimony for the reading of the text. Pilate provided a tribute to Jesus' kingship in a trilingual placard that everyone in Palestine could read,

for it was written in the three major languages of the day: Hebrew (or, Aramaic—the language of the Jews), Latin (the Roman language, the official language) and Greek (the *lingua franca*, the common tongue).

Textual Gap-filling: A variant reading is γεγραμμενον Εβραιστι, Ελληνιστι, Ρωμαιστι (written "in Hebrew, Greek, and Latin" in A Dˢ Θ f¹ Maj (so TR and KJV). A change in the order was made to accord with a geographical order going from East to West. This is scribal manipulation.

End of the Gospel

All MSS except *f*¹ conclude the gospel at 21:25. The story of the woman caught in adultery, traditionally placed at the end of John 7 (see note on John 7:53—8:11), is printed here (as in *f*¹) as follows:

⁵³ Each of them went home, ¹ while Jesus went to the Mount of Olives. ² Early in the morning he came to the temple. When the people came to him, he sat down and began to teach them. ³ The scribes and the Pharisees brought a woman who had been caught in adultery. Making her stand before all of them, ⁴ they told him, "Teacher, this woman was caught in the act of committing adultery. ⁵ The law of Moses commands us to stone such women. But what do you say?" ⁶ They were testing him, so as to bring some charge against him. Jesus bent down and with his finger wrote on the ground. ⁷ When they persisted in questioning him, he sat up and said to them, "Let him who is without sin be the first to throw a stone at her." ⁸ Once again he bent down and wrote on the ground. ⁹ When they heard this, they went away, one by one, beginning with the elders. Jesus was left alone with the woman standing before him. ¹⁰ Jesus sat up and said to her, "Woman, where are they now? Has anyone condemned you?" ¹¹ She answered, "No one, Lord." And Jesus replied, "Neither do I condemn you. Go your way, and don't sin again."

This is scribal gap-filling of a piece of oral tradition (see commentary above on John 7:53—8:11).

21:25

The word αμην (amen) is added in C² Θ Ψ *f* 13 Maj (so TR and KJV) by way of scribal gap-filling in the interest of oral reading in church.

Chapter Five

The Acts of the Apostles

Acts
3:6 | (added words in bold)
In the name of Jesus Christ, the Nazarene, **rise up and** walk.

Original Text: εν τω ονοματι Ιησου Χριστου του Ναζωραιου περιπατει (**in the name of Jesus Christ, the Nazarene, walk**). This is the original wording in the two earliest MSS (ℵ B) and D.
Textual Gap-filling: A variant reading adds εγειρε και, creating the rendering "rise up and walk" in A C E Ψ 095 33 1739 Maj (so TR and KJV), by way of scribal gap-filling.

3:13 | (added words in bold)
The God of Abraham, **the God** of Isaac, and **the God** of Jacob.

Original Text: ο θεος Αβρααμ και Ισαακ και Ιακωβ (**the God of Abraham, Isaac, and Jacob**). This is the original reading according to two early MSS (B 0236), as well as E 33 1739 Maj.
Textual Gap-filling: The name ο θεος is added two more times, creating the rendering, "the God of Abraham, the God of Isaac, and the God of Jacob" in four early MSS (ℵ A C D). This result of scribal gap-filling, making the reading more dramatic.

4:33 | (added word in bold)
the resurrection of the Lord Jesus **Christ**

Original Text: της αναστασεως του κυριου Ιησου (**the resurrection of the Lord Jesus**). This is the original reading according to two early MSS ($\mathfrak{P}^8$ B), as well as Maj syr[h] cop[sa].

Textual Gap-filling: The name is expanded by adding Χριστου (Christ), in two variants (1) "Lord Jesus Christ" in D E 1739, and (2) "Jesus Christ the Lord" in ℵ A. As often happened in the course of textual transmission, divine names were expanded by scribal gap-filling.

5:41 | (added words in bold)
suffer dishonor for the sake of the name **of Jesus**

Original Text: κατηξιωθησαν υπερ του ονοματος ατιμασθηναι (**suffer dishonor for the sake of the Name**). This is the original wording according to early and diverse testimony: $\mathfrak{P}^{74}$ ℵ A B C (D) 1739.

Textual Gap-filling: Scribes expanded "The Name" in three ways— by adding (1) αυτου, making it "his Name" (945 1175); (2) Ιησου, making it "the Name of Jesus" (Ψ 33 Maj; so KJV), and (3) κυριος Ιησου, making it "the Name of the Lord Jesus" (E). The absolute use of the term "the Name," referring to the all-inclusiveness of Jesus Christ's person, is spoiled here by the additions. The early Christians knew that "the Name" denoted "Jesus Christ." Other NT writers simply said "the Name" and expected their readers to know that this referred to Jesus Christ (see Heb 13:15; James 2:7; 3 John 7). Scribes sensed a gap in the text and filled it accordingly.

6:8 | (added words in bold)
full of grace, power, **faith, and the Spirit**

Original Text: χαριτος και δυναμεως (**grace and power**). This is the original wording according to early and diverse testimony: $\mathfrak{P}^8$ $\mathfrak{P}^{45\text{vid}}$ $\mathfrak{P}^{74}$ ℵ B D.

Textual Gap-filling: Several variations occur: χαριτος και πιστεως ("grace and faith") in E; πιστεως χαριτος και πνευματος ("faith, grace, and the Spirit") in Ψ; πιστεως και δυναμις ("faith and power") in Maj (so TR and KJV). All these are scribal alterations and expansions.

7:18 | (added words in bold)
another king **over Egypt**

Original Text: βασιλευς ετερος (**another king**). This is probably the original reading according to the earliest MS ($\mathfrak{P}^{45vid}$), as well as D E Maj.
Textual Gap-filling: A variant reading adds επ Αιγυπτον, creating the rendering "another king over Egypt"—in four early MSS (ℵ A B C), as well as $\mathfrak{P}^{33vid}$ $\mathfrak{P}^{74}$ Ψ. The textual evidence is divided; either reading could be original. But if the "text" is original, the variant is the product of scribal gap-filling, intending the clarify which king is being spoken about.

7:30 | (added words in bold)
angel **of the Lord**

Original Text: αγγελος (**angel**). This is the original wording according to four early MSS (ℵ A B C), as well as $\mathfrak{P}^{74}$.
Textual Gap-filling: A variant reading is αγγελος του κυριου ("angel of the Lord") in D E 33 1739 Maj (so TR and KJV), by way of scribal gap-filling—scribes making the identification of the Lord more certain.

8:36–38 | (added words in bold)
[36] Now as they were going along the road, they came to some water, and the eunuch said, "Look, there is water. What is to prevent me from being baptized? [37] **And Philip said, "If you believe with all your heart, you may. And he replied, "I believe that the Son of God is Jesus Christ."** [38] So he ordered the chariot to stop, and both Philip and the eunuch went down into water, and Philip baptized him.

The earliest and best Greek MSS ($\mathfrak{P}^{45}$ $\mathfrak{P}^{74}$ ℵ A B C), as well as syr[p] cop, do not include 8:37. Other MSS (4[mg] E 1739 it) add, And Philip said,

"If you believe with all your heart, you may. And he replied, "I believe that the Son of God is Jesus Christ." If the verse was an original part of Luke's text, there is no good reason for explaining why it would have been omitted in so many ancient MSS and versions. Rather, this verse is a classic example of scribal gap-filling, in that it supplied the apparent gap left by the unanswered question of the previous verse ("The eunuch said, 'Look, water! What could keep me from being baptized?'"). The interpolation puts an answer on Philip's lips that is derived from ancient Christian baptismal practices. Before being baptized, the new believer had to make a confession of his or her faith in Jesus as the Son of God. A similar addition also worked its way into the text of John 9:38–39 (see note). There is nothing doctrinally wrong with this interpolation; it affirms belief with the heart (in accordance with verses like Romans 10:9–10) and elicits the response of faith in Jesus Christ as the Son of God (in accordance with verses like John 20:31). But it is not essential that one make such a verbatim confession before being baptized. In fact, the eunuch had made no such confession, but it was obvious to Philip that he believed Jesus was the Christ when the eunuch said, "Look, water! What could prevent me from being baptized?" This is part of the beauty of the book of Acts: Many individuals come to faith in Christ in a variety of ways. The church throughout history has had a habit of standardizing the way people express their faith in Christ. It is difficult to know when this interpolation first entered the text, but it could have been as early as the second century, since Irenaeus (*Against Heresies* 3.12.8) quoted part of it. The earliest extant Greek manuscript to include is E, of the sixth century. Erasmus included the verse in his edition of the Greek New Testament because—even though it was not present in many of the MSS he knew—he considered it to have been omitted by the carelessness of scribes. He based its inclusion on a marginal reading in codex 4. From Erasmus' edition it worked its way into the TR and subsequently the KJV.

8:39 | (added words in bold)
the Holy Spirit fell upon the eunuch and an angel of the Lord raptured Philip

Original Text: πνευμα κυριου ηρπασεν τον Φιλιππον (**Spirit of Lord raptured Philip**). This is the original wording according to early MSS ($\mathfrak{P}^{45}$ ℵ A* B C), as well as $\mathfrak{P}^{74}$ E.

Textual Gap-filling: πνευμα αγιον επεπεσεν επι ευνουχον, αγγελος δε κυριος ηρπασεν τον Φιλιππον ("the Holy Spirit fell upon the eunuch and an angel of the Lord raptured Philip"). This is scribal gap-filling in A^c 1739, intended to say that the Holy Spirit fell on the eunuch after he was baptized (the usual Christian experience) and an angel snatched away Philip.

9:34 | (added words in bold)
the Lord Jesus Christ

Original Text: Ιησους Χριστος (**Jesus Christ**). This is the original wording according to three early MSS (ℵ B* C), as well as $\mathfrak{P}^{74}$.

Textual Gap-filling: Variant readings on the name are Ιησους ο Χριστος ("Jesus the Christ") in $\mathfrak{P}^{53vid}$ B^c E 1739 Maj (so TR and KJV) and ο κυριος Ιησους Χριστος ("the Lord Jesus Christ") in A. These expansions are simple scribal gap-filling, wherein the title of Jesus is expanded. This happens frequently in the New Testament textual transmission.

10:30 | (added words in bold)
I was **fasting and** praying

Original Text: προσευχομενος (**I was praying**). This is the original wording according to four early MSS (ℵ A* B C), as well as $\mathfrak{P}^{74}$.

Textual Gap-filling: A variant reading adds νηστευων και, creating the rendering, "I was fasting and praying" in $\mathfrak{P}^{50}$ A^2 (D). This is scribal gap-filling carried over from 10:10, where it says that Peter was hungry. So it was assumed by some scribe that he was fasting, and he added to the text accordingly.

11:12 | (added words in bold)
to accompany them **without hesitation [or, without distinction]**

Original Text: συνελθειν αυτοις (**to accompany them**). This is probably the original wording according to two early MSS (𝔓⁴⁵ᵛⁱᵈ D).

Textual Gap-filling: There are three variant readings, which have additions: (1) μηδεν διακριναντα, creating the rendering "to accompany them without making a distinction" (ℵ* A B E 33 1739), (2) μηδεν διακρινομεν, creating the rendering "to accompany them without hesitation" Maj (so TR and KJV), and (3) μηδεν ανακριναντα, creating the rendering "to accompany them without questioning" (𝔓⁷⁴), which are all likely the result of scribal gap-filling influenced by 10:20.

12:25 | (added words in bold)

having fulfilled their mission they returned **from** Jerusalem **to Antioch**

Original Text: υπεστρεψαν εις Ιερουσαλημ πληρωσαντες την διακονιαν (**having fulfilled their mission they returned to Jerusalem**). This is the original wording according to the two earliest MSS (ℵ B), as well as Maj copˢᵃ.

Textual Gap-filling: Other MSS add απο or εξ before "Jerusalem" (𝔓⁷⁴ A 33), creating the rendering, "they returned from Jerusalem, having completed their ministry"; still other MSS (E 1739) add εις Αντιοχειαν, creating the rendering "they returned from Jerusalem to Antioch, having completed their ministry." The reading in ℵ and B has to be translated as in the text above because Paul and Barnabas went to Jerusalem on a relief mission and then returned to Antioch. The other MSS make this clear by way of scribal gap-filling.

13:33 | (added words in bold)

it is written in the **second** [**or, first**] psalm

Original Text: τοις ψαλμοις (**the psalms**). This is the reading in the earliest MS (𝔓⁴⁵ᵛⁱᵈ).

Textual Gap-filling: Two variant readings show additions: (1) δευτερω ("second")—hence, "the second psalm" (𝔓⁷⁴ ℵ A B C) and (2) πρωτω ("first")—hence, "the first psalm" (D). The textual evidence is divided between "the psalms" found in the earliest MS (𝔓⁴⁵) and "the second psalm" found in other early MSS. Since the passage quoted is from Psalm 2:7, The reading "second" may be the result of scribal gap-filling in a scribal attempt to make the text accurate.

14:25 | (**added words in bold**)
the message **of the Lord** [**or, God**]

Original Text: τον λογον (**the message**). This is the original wording according to two early MSS (B D), as well as 1739 Maj.
Textual Gap-filling: Two variant readings are τον λογον του κυριου ("the message of the Lord") in ℵ A C 33, and τον λογον του θεου ("the message of God") in $\mathfrak{P}^{74}$ E. These are both the products of gap-filling, wherein scribes wanted to clarify the identity of "the message."

15:24 | (**added words in bold**)
commanded you **to be circumcised and keep the law**

Original text: εταραξαν υμας λογοις (**commanded you to do certain things**). This is the original wording according to early and diverse testimony: $\mathfrak{P}^{33}$ $\mathfrak{P}^{45vid}$ $\mathfrak{P}^{74}$ ℵ B D 33.
Textual Gap-filling: A variant reading adds λεγοντες περιτεμνεσθαι και τηρειν τον λογον (commanded you to be circumcised and keep the law) in C E 1739 Maj (so TR and KJV), by way of scribal expansion.

15:33–35 | (**added words in bold**)
[33] After they had spent some time there, they were sent off in peace by the brothers to those who had sent them. [34] **But it seemed good to Silas to remain there.** [35] But Paul and Barnabas remained in Antioch, teaching and proclaiming (along with many others) the message of the Lord.

Acts 15:34 is not included in many MSS, both early and diverse: $\mathfrak{P}^{74}$ ℵ A B E Ψ Maj syr^{p} cop^{bo}. The verse is added in two different forms in other MSS: (1) "But it seemed good to Silas to remain there" (C 33 1739 syr^{h**} cop^{sa}; so TR and KJV) (2) "But it seemed good to Silas to remain with them, so Judas traveled alone" ($\mathfrak{P}^{127vid}$ D). The extra verse, though it contradicts 15:33, was added to avoid the difficulty in 15:40, which indicates that Silas was still in Antioch. Thus, in trying to solve one problem, another was created. In any event, the additions are the products of scribal gap-filling.

16:31 | (added word in bold)
believe in the Lord Jesus **Christ**

Original Text: πιστευσον επι τον κυριον Ιησουν (**believe in the Lord Jesus**). This is the original wording according to early and excellent testimony: $\mathfrak{P}^{74\text{vid}}$ $\mathfrak{P}^{127}$ ℵ A B 33.
Textual Gap-filling: The name is "Lord Jesus Christ" (adding Χριστον) in C D E Ψ 1739 Maj syr cop^{sa} (so TR and KJV) by way of scribal gap-filling, expanding the title of Jesus.

18:21 | (added words in bold)
I must by all means make the festival in Jerusalem. I will return again.

Original Text: παλιν ανακαμψω (**I will return again**). This is the original wording according to three early MSS (ℵ A B), as well as $\mathfrak{P}^{74}$.
Textual Gap-filling: A variant reading addition is δει με παντως την εορτην την ερχομενην ποιησαι εις Ιερυσολυμα ("I must by all means make the festival in Jerusalem) in D Ψ Maj (so TR and KJV). Scribes filled a gap, adding these words to explain why Paul made such a hasty departure.

20:28 | (added words in bold)
the church **of the Lord and** God which he purchased with his own blood

Original Text: την εκκλησιαν του θεου ην περιεποισατο δια του αιματος του ιδιου (**the church of God which he purchased with his own blood**). This is the original wording according to the two earliest MSS (ℵ B), as well as cop^{boMS} syr.
Textual Gap-filling: "God" (θεου) is replaced with "Lord" (κυριου) in $\mathfrak{P}^{74}$ A C* D E 33 1739 cop, and "Lord and God" (κυριου και θεου)

in C[3] [ninth century] Maj. The reading "God," found in the two earliest MSS (א B), was likely changed to "Lord" because scribes were uncomfortable with the idea of God having blood. The second variant (Lord and God) is a conflation of the two readings. It is possible that the expression "with his own blood" could be rendered "the blood of his Own" or "the blood of his own Son." In other words, it is possible that Luke was thinking of "his own Son" when he wrote, "which God purchased with the blood of his own [του ιδιου]." In any event, the addition is the product of scribal gap-filling intended to fix an exegetical problem.

21:1 | **(added words in bold)**
they went to Patara **and Myra**

Text: Παταρα (Patara). This is the original wording according to four early MSS (א A B C), as well as 𝔓[74]. The documentary evidence supports the shorter reading.
Textual Gap-filling: This is expanded to "Patara and Myra" in 𝔓[41vid] D. Paul and his companions couldn't have reached Myra yet, which was another fifty miles away.

22:9 | **(added words in bold)**
they saw the light **and became afraid**

Original Text: το μεν φως εθεασαντο (**they saw the light**). This is the original wording according to three early MSS (א A B), as well as 𝔓[74] 049 33.
Textual Gap-filling: Scribes added και εμφοβοι εγενοντο creating the rendering "they saw the light and became afraid"—in D E Ψ 1739 Maj (so TR and KJV), by way of scribal gap-filling.

24:6–8 | **(added words in bold)**
[6] He even tried to desecrate the Temple, **so we arrested him, and we would have judged him according to our law,** [7] **but the commander Lysias came and with great force took him out of our hands,** [8] **commanding his accusers to come before you.** When you examine him

yourself, you will be able to learn from him about all these things we are accusing him of doing,

The best MSS ($\mathfrak{P}^{74}$ ℵ A B L) do not have the words in bold. The extra words (E Ψ Maj 33 1739; so TR and KJV) are the result of scribal gap-filling based on the previous narrative in Acts, which formed a horizon of expectation for this passage.

24:15 | (added words in bold)
there is going to be a resurrection **of the dead**

Original Text: αναστασιν μελλειν εσεσθαι (**there is going to be a resurrection**). This is the original wording according to four early MSS (ℵ A B C), as well as $\mathfrak{P}^{74}$ 33 1739.
Textual Gap-filling: Certain scribes added νεκρων, creating the rendering , "there is going to be a resurrection of the dead"—E Ψ Maj (so TR and KJV)—by way of scribal gap-filling.

28:28–29 | (added words in bold)
[28] Therefore, be advised that this salvation from God has been sent to the Gentiles, and they will listen. [29] **And after he said these things, the Jews went away, arguing greatly among themselves.**

The earliest and best Greek MSS ($\mathfrak{P}^{74}$ ℵ A B E 048 33 1739), as well as syr[p] and cop, do not include 28:29. It is added by way of narrative gap filling in the Majority of MSS (so TR and KJV).

28:31
A few MSS (Ψ and others) add αμην (amen) at the end of the book by way of scribal gap-filling in the interest of oral reading in church.

Chapter Six

Romans

Romans
5:2 | (added words in bold)
we have the access **by faith** into this grace

Original Text: την προσαγωγην εσχηκαμεν (**we have the access**). This is the original wording according to two early MSS (B 0220), as well as D F G cop^sa.
Textual Gap-filling: A variant reading adds τη πιστει creating the rendering, "we have access by faith" in two early MSS (ℵ* C), as well as 33 1739 Maj, by way of scribal gap-filling.

6:11 | (added words in bold)
alive to God in Christ Jesus **our Lord**

Original Text: Χριστω Ιησου (**Christ Jesus**). This is the original wording according to early and diverse testimony: 𝔓^46 A B D F G 1739*.
Textual Gap-filling: The name is expanded by adding τω κυριω ημων creating the title "Christ Jesus our Lord" in 𝔓^94vid ℵ C 33 1739^c Maj—scribal expansion of a divine name (common in the NT Epistles), perhaps influenced by 5:21; 6:23.

8:23 | (added words in bold)
eagerly expecting **sonship**, the redemption of our bodies

Original Text: απεκδεχομενοι την απολυτρωσιν του σωματος ημων (**eagerly expecting the redemption of our bodies**). This is the wording in the two earliest MSS ($\mathfrak{P}^{27vid}$ $\mathfrak{P}^{46}$), as well as D F G.

Textual Gap-filling: A variant reading adds υιοθεσιαν creating the rendering, "eagerly expecting sonship, the redemption of our bodies" in four early MSS (א A B C), as well as 33 1739 Maj. Final redemption understood as "sonship" will occur when Christians get resurrected bodies.

8:26 | (added words in bold)
the Spirit intercedes **on our behalf**

Original Text: το πνευμα υπερεντυγχανει (**the Spirit intercedes**). This is the original wording according to six early MSS ($\mathfrak{P}^{27vid}$ $\mathfrak{P}^{46vid?}$ א* A B D), as well as F G 1739.

Textual Gap-filling: A variant reading adds υπερ ημων creating the rendering, "intercedes on our behalf" in א² [seventh century] C 33 Maj (so TR and KJV). This is scribal gap-filling of what would naturally follow the verb "intercedes."

8:34 | (added words in bold)
he rose again **from the dead**

Original Text: εγερθεις (**he rose again**). This is the original wording according to the three earliest MSS ($\mathfrak{P}^{27vid}$ $\mathfrak{P}^{46}$ B), as well as א² [seventh century] D F G 33 Maj.

Textual Gap-filling: A variant reading adds εκ νεκρων creating the rendering "rose again from the dead" in three early MSS (א* A C), as well as 0289^{vid}. Clearly the addition is the product of scribal gap-filling supplying a prepositional phrase after the verb.

11:6 | (added words in bold)

grace would no longer be grace. **But if it is of works, then it is no longer grace; otherwise work is no longer work.**

Original text: η χαρις ουκετι γινεται χαρις (**grace would no longer be grace**). This is the original wording in four early MSS ($\mathfrak{P}^{46}$ ℵ* A C), as well as D F G 1739 cop.

Textual Gap-filling: A variant reading adds ει δε εξ εργων ουκετι εστι χαρις επει το εργον ουκετι εστιν εργον (but if it is of works, then it is no longer grace; otherwise work is no longer work). This addition is in one early MS (B), as well as ℵ² [seventh century] 33^vid Maj (so TR and KJV). The textual evidence in favor of the shorter reading is impressive. Furthermore, there is no good reason to account for the omission of the second sentence (in the variant) had it been originally in the epistle. Thus, the variant is likely an interpolation created perhaps as early as the fourth century. But this gloss does not help elucidate the passage, which plainly depicts the nature of grace as being a free gift, not a reward for doing work. The scribal gap-filling adds nothing to this, but rather detracts with the opaque statement, "otherwise work is no longer work."

11:17 | (added words in bold)

the root of the richness of the olive tree

Original Text: της πιοτητος της ελαιας εγενου (**the richness of the olive tree**). This is the original reading according to the earliest MS ($\mathfrak{P}46$), as well as D* F G cop^bo.

Textual Gap-filling: Two variant readings add της ριζης in (1) "the root of the richness of the olive tree" (ℵ* B C), and (2) "the root and the richness of the olive tree" (ℵ² A D² 33 1739 Maj; so TR and KJV)—both scribal gap-fillers carried over from 11:16 where "the root" is mentioned.

13:9 | (added words in bold)
do not steal, **do not bear false witness,** do not covet

Original Text: ου κλεψεις (**do not steal**). This is the original wording according to three early MSS ($\mathfrak{P}^{46}$ A B), as well as D F G L 1739.
Textual Gap-filling: A variant reading adds, ου ψευδομαρτυρησεις (do not bear false witness) in one early MS (‭א‬), as well as 048. This is clearly scribal gap-filing, wherein a scribe wanted this text to be as complete as what is found in the Ten Commandments (see Exod 20:15–17)

14:6 | (added words in bold)
those who observe a certain day do so to the Lord; **and those who don't observe a certain day also do so to the Lord**

Original Text: ο φρονων την ημεραν κυριω φρονει (**those who observe a certain day do so to the Lord**). This is the original wording according to five early MSS ($\mathfrak{P}^{46}$ ‭א‬ A B, as well as C^{2vid} [sixth century] D F G 048 1739.
Textual Gap-filling: A variant reading repeats this clause in the negative: "and those who don't observe a certain day also do so to the Lord" in later MSS (C^3 [ninth century] 33 Maj; so TR and KJV). This is a scribal gap-filler.

14:23
The doxology that appears as 16:25–27 in most MSS is included here in A P 33 both at the end of chapter 14 and at the end of chapter 16. It is added here only in Ψ 0209^{vid} Maj MSS$^{according\ to\ Origen}$. The doxology also appears at the end of chapter 15 in the earliest MS, $\mathfrak{P}^{46}$ (see extensive notes on 15:33 and 16:23 for discussion).

15:29 | the full blessing of Christ
This is the original wording according to five early MSS ($\mathfrak{P}^{46}$ ‭א‬* A B C), as well as 1739. Two variant readings are "the full blessing of the gospel of Christ" (‭א‬^{2} 33 Maj; so TR and KJV), and "the full assurance of the blessing of Christ" (D* F G). The text has the support of the five earliest MSS.

15:31 | my ministry

This is the original wording according to three early MSS ($\mathfrak{P}^{46}$ ℵ C), as well as D¹ 33 1739 Maj. A variant reading is, "my bringing of a gift" in one early MS (B), as well as D* F G. The variant is a scribal attempt to explain that Paul's ministry (or, service) to Jerusalem was the bringing of a (monetary) gift.

15:33 plus 16:25–27 | (the concluding doxology)

The earliest MS, $\mathfrak{P}^{46}$ (dated mid-second century), concludes chapter 15 with a four-verse doxology: 15:33 followed by what is normally printed as 16:25–27. $\mathfrak{P}^{46}$, with its doxology after 15:32, probably reflects a form of the epistle that originally had only fifteen chapters, to which chapter sixteen (a separate, accompanying letter) was later appended. $\mathfrak{P}^{46}$ shows a very primitive form of the Pauline text and corpus as a whole (see Comfort & Barrett, *Text of Earliest NT Greek MSS*, 204–206). As to Romans, $\mathfrak{P}^{46}$ could very well reflect a form of the epistle as compiled by an early editor of Paul's epistles—that is, one who placed and arranged Paul's epistles in one codex. This compiler could have seamed together Paul's original complete epistle from 1:1–15:32, which ends with his four-verse doxology (15:33 with what is usually printed as 16:25–27, concluded with a final "amen") and the appended letter of recommendation (chapter 16)—which in $\mathfrak{P}^{46}$ does not have a final benediction. Rather, it ends with a final greeting from Erastus and Quartus (16:23). So the arrangement in $\mathfrak{P}^{46}$ is as follows: (a) 1:1–15:32; (b) 15:33 + 16:25–27, the doxology—concluded with "amen"; (c) 16:1–23, a short letter with recommendations for Phoebe and greetings for and from several believers. The fact that $\mathfrak{P}^{46}$ (with A F G) does not have an "amen" at the end of 15:33 means that 15:33 is immediately followed by the doxology (usually printed as 16:25–27) and becomes the first part of it, as reflected in this translation. As in many doxologies, Paul elevated his language beyond normal prose into poetry. This poetic doxology is syntactically balanced by the three-time occurrence of the Greek preposition *kata* (translated here as "according to"). For further discussion on the doxology, see note on 16:23.

16:23

The earliest manuscript, $\mathfrak{P}^{46}$ (mid-second century), ends the book of Romans at the end of 16:23 and immediately begins with the book of Hebrews. The doxology (normally printed as 16:25–27) appears at the end of chpt. 15 in $\mathfrak{P}^{46}$ (see note there). Some MSS (see below) add a verse here (16:24), as follows: "The grace of our Lord Jesus Christ be with you all. Amen." Several other MSS add the doxology of 16:25–27 (see note on 15:33).

The various placements of the doxology in the extant MSS are as follows: (1) 1:1–16:23 + doxology ($\mathfrak{P}^{61vid?}$ ℵ B C D 1739 it[d] syr[p] cop [Note: the first extant page of $\mathfrak{P}^{61}$ exhibits portions of Romans 16:23, with 16:24 vacant, and 16:25–26. Thus, it is certain that the doxology immediately followed 16:23. What is not certain is whether or not $\mathfrak{P}^{61}$ also had the doxology at the end of Romans 14 and/or 15]); (2) 1:1–15:32 + 15:33 and doxology + 16:1–23 ($\mathfrak{P}^{46}$); (3) 1:1–14:23 + doxology + 15:1–16:23 + doxology (A P 33); (4) 1:1–14:23 + doxology + 15:1–16:24 (L Ψ 0209[vid] syr[h] MSS[according to Origen] [Origen is said to have known MSS that included the doxology after 14:23]; (5) 1:1–16:24 (F G MSS[according to Jerome] [in Codex G, the scribe left a space after 14:23 large enough to contain the doxology, intimating that he knew of MSS that placed it after 14:23 but that it was not so in his exemplar. Jerome indicated he knew of various MSS that did not contain the doxology]); (6) 1:1–14:23 Marcion[according to Origen] [According to Rufunius' translation of Origen's *Commentary on Romans* 8.453, Origen said Marcion not only deleted 16:25–27, but also all of chapters 15–16); (7) 1:1–14:23 + 16:24 + doxology (Vulgate MSS (1648 1792 2089) Codex Amiatinus[vid]; (8) 1:1–16:23 + 16:24 + doxology (Maj, so TR); (9) 1:1–14:23 + doxology + 15:1–33 + doxology + 16:1–23 (1506).

The various placements of the doxology in the last chapters of Romans, as well as the content of chapter 15 and especially chapter 16, have caused textual critics and biblical scholars to ask many questions about the arrangement of Paul's epistle to the Romans. Did it originally have only 14 chapters, to which two more were added? Or did it originally have only 15 chapters, to which the sixteenth was added? Or was it a sixteen-chapter epistle from the very beginning? And to which of these chapters does the doxology belong? As to the position that Romans was originally only fourteen chapters, there is no actual Greek manuscript evidence to support this. What we have is Origen's comment that Marcion's edition of Romans ended at chapter fourteen (#6 above), and there are some clues in a few Latin MSS that this may have been so (#7 and see comments below).

If Origen's words about Marcion's deletion can be trusted (see Westcott and Hort, *The New Testament in the Original Greek, Introduction and Appendix,* 111–113, who have their doubts that Origen meant that all of chapters 15–16 were deleted by Marcion), then it is possible that the purported MSS ending with 14:23 or having the doxology there (#4, #6, #7) reflect Marcion's influence. (The readings #3 and #9 may also reflect this influence, but not fully.) Marcion would have been prone to delete chapter 15 because (1) it says that "whatever was written in former days was written for our instruction" (15:4); (2) it calls Christ "a servant to the circumcised to show God's truthfulness, to confirm the promises given to the patriarchs" (15:8); and (3) it is full of OT quotations (15:9–12). F. F. Bruce (*The Letter of Paul to the Romans*, 29) said, "such a concentration of material offensive to Marcion can scarcely be paralleled in the Pauline writings." It is possible that Marcion would not need to delete chapter 16 because it might not have been known to him.

The chapter summaries or *capitula* in Codex Amiatinus suggest that 16:25–27 immediately followed 14:1–23 in archetypal MSS. *Capitula* 50 reads "concerning the danger of grieving one's brother with one's food, and showing that the kingdom of God is not food and drink but righteousness and peace and joy in the Holy Spirit," followed by *capitula* 51: "concerning the mystery of God, which was kept in silence before the passion but has been revealed after his passion." Gamble (*The Textual History of the Letter to the Romans*, 1977, 132–133) argues for the original positioning of the doxology at 14:23 because putting the doxology at 16:23–25 would violate Paul's normal pattern of a grace benediction appearing at the close of the epistle. At the same time, Gamble argues for the inclusion of 16:24, but this has weak textual support (see #4 above).

Whatever one supposes about the epistle originally ending with chapter 14, the textual evidence stands against it. All extant Greek MSS have chapters 14, 15, and 16. Chapter fifteen is completely contiguous with chapter fourteen, and it is replete with Pauline thought—the likes of which only Marcion would object to. The sixteenth chapter is different in intent and content. The epistle does not need it for any kind of completion inasmuch as Paul came to a natural conclusion in 15:30–33, where he asks the believers for their prayers, especially in anticipation of his coming to them, and then concludes with a benediction: "May the God of peace be with you all. Amen."

What we know as Romans 16 may have been sent as a separate letter of recommendation for Phoebe (with personal greetings included), which was later attached to the rest of the epistle. Or Paul may have made two copies of the epistle, one with chapter 16 (which may have gone to Ephesus) and one without chapter 16 (which would have gone to Rome). Interestingly, Codex G does not include "in Rome" in Romans 1:7 and 15, and also has all sixteen chapters without a doxology. Some have thought that this codex could be a witness to an earlier form of the epistle that would not have gone to the Romans (see #5 above). However, the subscription in G indicates that the letter was sent to the Romans.

$\mathfrak{P}^{46}$, with its doxology after 15:32 (see #2 above), probably reflects a form of the epistle that originally had only fifteen chapters, to which chapter 16 (a separate, accompanying letter) was later appended. $\mathfrak{P}^{46}$, dated in the middle of the second century, shows a very primitive form of the Pauline text and corpus as a whole (see Comfort & Barrett, *Text of Earliest NT Greek MSS*, 204–206). As to Romans, $\mathfrak{P}^{46}$ could very well reflect a form of the epistle as compiled by an early editor of Paul's epistles—that is, one who placed and arranged Paul's epistles in one codex. This compiler could have seamed together Paul's original complete epistle from 1:1–15:32 (which ends with his four-verse doxology [15:33 + 16:25–27] and a final "amen") and the accompanying letter of recommendation (chapter 16)—which in $\mathfrak{P}^{46}$ does not have a final benediction. Rather, it ends with a final greeting from Erastus and Quartus (16:23). So the arrangement in $\mathfrak{P}^{46}$ is as follows: 1:1–15:32; 15:33 + 16:25–27, the four-verse doxology—concluded with "amen"; 16:1–23 a short letter with recommendations for Phoebe and greetings from several believers.

The double presence of the doxology in certain MSS (A P 33, see #3)—both at the end of chapter 14 and of chapter 16—indicates that by the fifth century (and thereafter) some scribes were seeing the doxology at the end of both chapters in various exemplars and then copied it accordingly. The same holds true for the scribe of 1509, who must have seen the doxology at the end of chapter 15 (as in $\mathfrak{P}^{46}$) and at the end of chapter 16 (as in several MSS) in certain exemplars.

Some scholars think Paul wrote all sixteen chapters as one unit, which he concluded with his doxology at the end of chapter 16 (as in #1 above). This was then abridged to a fifteen-chapter epistle when it was circulated to other churches, because these churches would not need or be interested in the circumstantial details of chapter 16. But since there is not one extant manuscript that ends with chapter 15, this view has no textual support.

In conclusion, it seems to me that the presence of the doxology appearing at the end of chapter 14 only (as in #4) reflects the influence of Marcion. The presence of the doxology at the end of chapter 16 reflects the work of a compiler (or compilers) who moved it there when they added chapter sixteen to the main body of the letter. The most likely original arrangement is reflected in $\mathfrak{P}^{46}$ (the earliest manuscript), which has the doxology at the end of chapter 15, to which is appended an extra chapter, which probably was a short letter sent along to Rome with the major epistle (Rom 1–15)—much in the same way that Paul's letter to Philemon was sent along with his letter to the Colossians. Since this short letter begins with Paul's recommendation of Phoebe, it could very well be that Phoebe carried both epistles (Rom 1–15; Rom 16) to the leaders of the church in Rome. This letter of recommendation includes several personal greetings and its own short benediction: "the grace of our Lord Jesus be with you" (16:20). In keeping with his usual practice, Paul probably wrote this benediction in his own hand (see Comfort, *Encountering the Manuscripts*, 2005, 7–8), as well as the next verse, where he passes on the greetings of "Timothy, my co-worker" (16:21). Tertius, the amanuensis of this final chapter and probably of all Romans, signed off his own hand (16:22). He may have also passed along greetings from Gaius, Erastus, and Quartus—or, as is in keeping with ancient letter writing, each of these men gave their greeting in their own handwriting (16:23). As such, at the close of the original letter, the Roman Christians would see several different signatures. After this, they would not see the doxology; they would see blank papyrus.

In the final analysis, it is probable that 16:24 (so TR and KJV) is clearly a scribal addition and that 16:25–27 was added after the epistle was penned and edited to include chapter 16, which is an appended chapter. In short, Paul did not write 16:24–27; it was added by later scribes when chapter sixteen was added to the rest of the epistle.

Chapter Seven

First Corinthians

First Corinthians
1:8 | (added word in bold)
the day of our Lord Jesus **Christ**

Original Text: τη ημερα του κυριου ημων Ιησου (**the day of our Lord Jesus**). This is the original wording according to the two earliest MSS ($\mathfrak{P}^{46}$ B).
Textual Gap-filling: The name is expanded by adding Χριστου to make it "Lord Jesus Christ" in ℵ A C D F G 33 1739 Maj syr cop (so TR and KJV), a carryover from 1:7 where the name is "Lord Jesus Christ."

1:14 | (added word in bold)
I thank **God**

Original Text: ευχαριστω (**I am thankful**). This is the original wording according to the two earliest MSS (ℵ* B).
Textual Gap-filling: Two variant readings add τω θεω: "I thank God" (ℵ² C D F G Maj; so TR and KJV), and "I thank my God" (A 33), both scribal expansions.

2:4 | (added words in bold)
persuasive **words of** wisdom

Original Text: πειθοις σοφιας (**persuasive wisdom**) This is the original wording according to the earliest MS ($\mathfrak{P}^{46}$), as well as F G.

Textual Gap-filling: A variant reading adds λογοις, creating the rendering, "persuasive words of wisdom" in two early MSS (**א*** B), as well as D 33 1739, by way of scribal gap-filling.

5:5 | (added words in bold)
the day of the Lord **Jesus Christ**

Original Text: τη ημερα του κυριου (**the day of the Lord**). This is the original wording according to the two earliest MSS ($\mathfrak{P}^{46}$ B), as well as 1739.

Textual Gap-filling: The title is expanded to "Lord Jesus" in $\mathfrak{P}^{61vid}$ **א** Ψ Maj (adding Ιησου) and "Lord Jesus Christ" in A D F G (adding Ιησου Χριστου).

5:7 | (added words in bold)
Christ our Passover Lamb has been sacrificed **for us**

Original Text: το πασχα ημων ετυθη Χριστος (**Christ our Passover Lamb has been sacrificed**). This is the original wording according to five early MSS ($\mathfrak{P}^{46vid}$ **א*** A B C*), as well as $\mathfrak{P}^{11vid}$ D F G 33 1739.

Textual Gap-filling: Another wording adds υπερ ημων, creating the rendering "Christ our Passover Lamb has been sacrificed for us") in later MSS (**א²** [seventh century] C³ [ninth century] Ψ Maj; so TR and KJV), by way of scribal expansion. (The *editio principes* of $\mathfrak{P}^{46}$ did not reconstruct this portion of the manuscript, but it is reconstructed in Comfort & Barrett, *Text of Earliest NT Greek MSS*, 257.)

7:5 | (added words in bold)
devote yourselves to **fasting and** prayer

Original Text: σχολασητε τη προσευχη (**devote yourselves to prayer**). This is the original wording according to early and diverse MSS: $\mathfrak{P}^{11vid}$ $\mathfrak{P}^{46}$ **א*** A B C D F G Ψ 1739 cop.

Textual Gap-filling: A variant reading adds νηστεια και creating the reading "devote yourselves to fasting and prayer" in ℵ² [seventh century] Maj syr (so TR and KJV), by way of scribal gap-filling perhaps influenced by a variant in Mark 9:29 (see note there).

11:24 | (added words in bold)
take, eat, this is my body **broken** for you

Original Text: μου εστιν το σωμα το υπερ υμων (this is my body for you). This is the original wording according to five early MSS (𝔓⁴⁶ ℵ* A B C*), as well as 1739*.
Textual Gap-filling: A variant reading in later MSS are "take, eat, this is my body broken for you" (adding λαβετε, φαγετε and κλωμενον) in C³ [ninth century] Ψ Maj (so TR and KJV), the product of scribal gap-filling influenced by Jesus' words in Matthew 26:26.

11:29a | (added word in bold)
whoever eats and drinks **unworthily**, eats and drinks judgment to himself

Original Text: ο γαρ εσθιων και πινων κριμα εαυτω εσθιει και πινει (**whoever eats and drinks, eats and drinks judgment on himself**). This is the original wording according to five early MSS (𝔓⁴⁶ ℵ* A B C*), as well as 1739 cop.
Textual Gap-filling: A variant reading of the first phrase adds αναξιως, creating the reading "whoever eats and drink unworthily" in ℵ² [seventh century] Cᶜ D F G Maj syr (so TR and KJV), by way of scribal gap-filling, attempting to make clear what is already evident in the context.

11:29b | (added words in bold)
not discerning the body **of the Lord**

Original Text: μη διακρινων το σωμα (**not discerning the body**). This is the original wording according to five early MSS (𝔓⁴⁶ ℵ* A B C*), as well as 1739 cop.

Textual Gap-filling: A variant reading adds του κυριου creating the rendering, "not discerning the body of the Lord" in ℵ² [seventh century] Cᶜ D F G Maj syr (so TR and KJV), by way of scribal gap-filling clarifying that the text is speaking of Jesus' body, not the church as the body of Christ.

14:34–35

Some MSS (D F G itᵃ,ᵇ) place these verses after 14:40, prompting some scholars to deem these verses as a gloss that was added into the text (see full discussion in *NT Text and Translation Commentary*, 518–519). But the earliest MSS (𝔓⁴⁶ ℵ A B) place the verses after 14:33.

15:54 | (added words in bold)

when the perishable puts on the imperishable and when the mortal puts on immortality

Original Text: και το θνητον τουτο ενδυσηται αθανασιαν (**when this mortal puts on immortality**) This is the wording according to three early MSS (𝔓⁴⁶ ℵ* C*), as well as 088 0243 1739* it copᵇᵒ.

Textual Gap-filling: A variant reading adds before the text οταν δε το φθαρτον τουτο ενδυσηται αφθαρσιαν (when this perishable puts on the imperishable). This appears in later MSS: ℵ² [seventh century] (A) B C²ᵛⁱᵈ [sixth century] D (33) 1739ᶜ Maj (so TR and KJV). This gap-filling elongates the statement for dramatic effect.

16:24

The word αμην (amen) was added in several MSS (ℵ A C D Ψ Maj; so TR and KJV) by way of scribal gap-filling. The addition was made in the interest of oral reading in the church.

Chapter Eight

Second Corinthians

Second Corinthians
1:13 | (added words in bold)
for we did not write to you anything other than what you can read **and**
understand

Original Text: ου γαρ αλλα γραφομεν υμιν αλλ η α αναγινωσκετε
(**we did not write to you anything other than what you can read**) . This
is the original wording according to the two earliest MSS ($\mathfrak{P}^{46}$ B).
Textual Gap-filling: Most other MSS add to this η και επιγινωσκετε
(and what you can know) creating the rendering, "we did not write to
you anything other than what you can read and what you can know"—a
product of scribal gap-filling.

4:14 | (added words in bold)
the one who raised up **the Lord** Jesus

Original Text: ο εγειρας τον Ιησουν (**the one who raised Jesus**).
This is the original wording according to the two earliest MSS ($\mathfrak{P}^{46}$ B),
as well as 0243 33 1739.
Textual Gap-filling: A variant reading adds κυριον (Lord) in $\aleph$ C D F
G Ψ Maj (so TR and KJV), by way of scribal expansion.

10:1 | Now I, Paul, appeal to you personally
It is possible that Paul took pen (stylus) in hand and began to write the rest of the epistle (see 13:10), as he did in other epistles (Gal 6:11–18; 2 Thess 3:17–18). Some scholars think chapters 10–13 are a separate epistle, perhaps "the sorrowful letter" that Paul refers to in 7:8, which was then appended to the end of chapter 9 by some editor early in the textual history of Paul's epistles.

13:13
The word αμην (amen) was added in several MSS (ℵ² D Ψ Maj; so TR and KJV) by way of scribal gap-filling. The addition was made in the interest of oral reading in the church.

Chapter Nine

Galatians

Galatians
1:8–9
Based on line lengths and page length, it is likely that 𝔓⁴⁶ did not include 1:9, which reads, "As we have just said, and now say again, if anyone proclaims a message besides that which you received, let that one be cursed!" (For reconstruction of the text of 𝔓⁴⁶ here, see Comfort & Barrett, *Text of Earliest NT Greek MSS*, 313). If 𝔓⁴⁶ retains the original text, then the addition of 1:9 was added via scribal gap-filling to enhance dramatic effect—Paul repeating almost verbatim what he uttered in 1:8.

1:15 | (added words in bold)
When it pleased **God**, the One separating from the womb, **and calling me by his grace**

Original Text: οτε δε ευδοκησεν ο αφορισας με εκ κοιλιας μητρος μου (**when it pleased the One separating me from my mother's womb**). This is probably the original wording according to the earliest MS (𝔓⁴⁶), as well as 1739 1881.
Textual Gap-filling: A variant reading adds, "God" (θεος) and the phrase "and called me by his grace" (και καλεσας δια της χατριτος αυτου) in ℵ A B D F G Ψ 33 Maj (so TR and KJV)—probably scribal gap-filling.

3:21 | (added words in bold)
the promises **of God**

Original Text: των επαγγελιων (**the promises**). This is the original wording according to the two earliest MSS ($\mathfrak{P}^{46}$ B).
Textual Gap-filling: A variant reading adds του θεου creating the reading "the promises of God" in ℵ A C D (F G) Ψ 33 1739 Maj (so TR and KJV), by way of scribal gap-filling.

5:24 | (added word in bold)
the ones belonging to Christ **Jesus**

Original Text: οι δε του Χριστου (**the ones belonging to Christ**). This is the original wording according to the earliest MS ($\mathfrak{P}^{46}$), as well as D F G 0122 Maj.
Textual Gap-filling: The divine name is filled out by adding Ιησου making the reading "Christ Jesus" in ℵ A B C 33 1739, by way of scribal gap-filling, expanding the divine title.

6:15 | (added words in bold)
for in Christ Jesus neither circumcision nor uncircumcision [counts]

Original Text: ουτε γαρ περιτομη τι εστιν ουτε ακροβυστια (for neither circumcision or uncircumcision [counts]) This is the original wording in the two earliest MSS ($\mathfrak{P}^{46}$ B), as well as Ψ 33 1739.
Textual Gap-filling: A variant reading adds εν γαρ Χριστω Ιησου, creating the rendering "for in Christ Jesus neither circumcision nor uncircumcision counts for anything" in three early MSS (ℵ A C), as well as D F G Maj (so TR and KJV), by way of scribal gap-filling influenced by 5:6.

Chapter Ten

Ephesians

Ephesians
1:1 | (added words in bold)
to those **in Ephesus** who are holy

Original text: τοις αγιοις τοις ουσιν (**to those who are holy**). This is the original wording according to the three earliest MSS ($\mathfrak{P}^{46}$ ℵ* B), as well as 1739.
Textual Gap-filling: A variant reading adds εν Εφεσω adds "to those in Ephesus who are holy" in ℵ² [seventh century] A B² [tenth century] D F G Ψ 0278 33 Maj it syr cop (so TR and KJV). According to the evidence of the three earliest MSS, it is obvious that "in Ephesus" was added later in the textual transmission of this letter. The truth is, the epistle known as "Ephesians" was as an encyclical intended for the audience of several churches—likely those in Asia Minor, the same seven churches in Revelation 1:11 (Ephesus, Smyrna, Pergamum, Thyatira, Sardis, Philadelphia, Laodecia), plus Hierapolis and Colossae. The epistle known as "Ephesians," in its content, has all the earmarks of being an encyclical. First, there are no personal exchanges and greetings, which one would expect because Paul had lived in Ephesus for two years. Second, Paul didn't deal with any local situations or problems, which he did in every other epistle. Third, the content of the epistle, especially with regard to the church, is universal in scope. Fourth, in 2:19

Paul spoke of the recipients as being "the households [plural, οικειοι] of God," very likely referring to several local churches. Fifth, when Paul told the Colossians to read the epistle coming from Laodicea (Col 4:16), he must have been referring to the epistle known as Ephesians, an encyclical. Tychicus delivered both the epistle known as "Ephesians" and the epistle to Colossians to these churches (Eph 6:21–22; Col 4:7–9). The words "in Ephesus" were added because Ephesus was the leading church in the province.

This product of gap-filling fits well, grammatically speaking, after the words τοις ουσιν (the ones being). But so would any other prepositional phrase with a location in Asia Minor like "in Colossae" or "in Philadelphia"—which was likely what happened as the epistle circulated. It just so happens that the one that was popular in later MSS was "in Ephesus."

1:15 | (added words in bold)
your trust in the Lord Jesus **and love** for all the holy believers

Original Text: υμας πιστιν εν τω κυριω Ιησου και την παντας τους αγιους (**your trust in the Lord Jesus and in all the holy believers**). This is the original wording according to the four earliest MSS ($\mathfrak{P}^{46}$ $\aleph$* A B), as well as 33 1739.

Textual Gap-filling: A variant reading adds την αγαπην creating the rendering, "your trust in the Lord Jesus and love for all the holy believers" in $\aleph^2$ [seventh century] D² Ψ Maj (so TR and KJV). The text has superior documentation. Paul was commending the believers for trusting Jesus and other believers. Certain scribes thought it odd that Paul would speak of trusting Jesus *and* the believers so they added "love for all the believers."

4:9a | (added word in bold)
he descended **first**

Original text: κατεβη (**he descended**). This is the original wording according to early and diverse testimony: $\mathfrak{P}^{46}$ $\aleph$* A C* D F G I^{vid}.

Textual Gap-filling: A variant reading adds πρωτον creating the rendering "he descended first" in ℵ² [seventh century] B C³ [ninth century] Ψ Maj (so TR and KJV), by way of scribal gap-filling.

4:9b | (added word in bold)
lower **parts** of the earth

Original Text: εις τα κατωτερα της γης (**into the lower earth**). This is the reading according to the earliest MS (𝔓⁴⁶), as well as D* F G. **Textual Gap-filling:** A variant reading adds μερη creating the rendering, "to the lower parts of the earth" in ℵ A B C D² I Ψ 33 1739 Maj. Both readings have good support; either reading could be original. The first reading speaks of Christ's descent to earth via incarnation. The second reading could speak of Christ's descent into the underworld between his burial and resurrection (see 1 Pet 3:18–19)—to make a parallel statement to that which follows ("ascended above all the heavens"). Thus, the variant is suspect as a product of scribal gap-filling.

5:5 | (added words in bold)
the kingdom of **Christ and** God

Original Text: τη βασιλεια του θεου (**the kingdom of God**). This is the reading in the earliest MS (𝔓⁴⁶). The additions that follow show that this is the most likely original wording.
Textual Gap-filling: Other readings are "kingdom of God and Christ" (F G), "kingdom of the Christ of God" (1739), and "kingdom of Christ and God" (ℵ A B Maj; so TR and KJV). The shortest reading in 𝔓⁴⁶ could be original—the other readings being scribal expansions.

5:19 | (added word in bold)
psalms, hymns, and **spiritual** songs

Original Text: ψαλμοις και υμνοις και ωδαις (**psalms, hymns, and songs**). "Songs" is probably the original wording according to the two earliest MSS (𝔓⁴⁶ B).

Textual Gap-filling: The word πνευματικαις (spiritual) was added to make it conform with the previous statement about "being filled with the Spirit." Two variants are "spiritual songs" (ℵ D F G Ψ 0278 33 1739 Maj it syr cop), and "spiritual songs with grace" (A) by way of scribal conformity to Colossians 3:16, a parallel verse.

5:22 | (added words in bold)
the wives **should submit** to their own husbands

Original Text: αι γυναικες τοις ιδιοις ανδρασιν (**the wives to their own husbands**). This is the original wording according to the two earliest MSS (𝔓⁴⁶ B), as well as Clement MSS^according to Jerome. The text has the earliest testimony (𝔓⁴⁶ B Clement).

Textual Gap-filling: A variant reading adds υποτασσεσθε creating the rendering "the wives should submit to their own husbands" in ℵ A I P 0278 33 1739. This is the product of a scribe or scribes adding a verb to make the statement have better sense.

6:19 | (added words in bold)
that I may boldly make known the mystery **of the gospel**

Original Text: το μυστηρον (**the mystery**). "Mystery" is the original wording according to the two earliest MSS (𝔓^{46vid} B), as well as F G it^b. The reconstruction of the lines in 𝔓⁴⁶ allow for "mystery" to fit the space as opposed to "mystery of the gospel."

Textual Gap-filling: A variant reading adds του ευαγγελιου, creating the rendering "the mystery of the gospel" in ℵ A D I Ψ 0278 33 1739 Maj syr cop (so TR and KJV), probably by way of scribal expansion. But Paul's mystery wasn't just the gospel, it was the mystery of Christ and the church— Jewish Christians and Gentile Christians being one body (3:4–7; 5:32).

6:24
The word αμην (amen) was added in several MSS (ℵ² D Ψ Maj; so TR and KJV) by way of scribal gap-filling. The addition was made in the interest of oral reading in the church.

Chapter Eleven

Philippians

Philippians
1:14 | (added words in bold)
the message **of God [or, the Lord]**

Original Text: τον λογον (**the message**). This is the original wording according to the earliest MS ($\mathfrak{P}^{46}$), as well as D² 1739 Maj.
Textual Gap-filling: Two variants are "the message of God" (adding θεου) in ℵ A B D* P 048^{vid} 33), and "the message of the Lord" (adding κυριου) in F G, both the products of scribal gap-filling intended to fill out the expression.

3:13 | (added word in bold)
I do not consider myself to have laid hold **yet.**

Original Text: ου λογιζομαι κατειληφεναι (**I do not consider myself to have laid hold**). This is the original wording according to the two earliest MSS ($\mathfrak{P}^{46}$ B), as well as D² F G Ψ Maj.
Textual Gap-filling: A variant reading adds ουπω creating the rendering, "I do not consider myself to have laid hold yet" in $\mathfrak{P}^{61vid}$ ℵ A D* P 33, by way of scribal gap-filling—holding out the potential that Paul could one day lay hold of the prize.

4:13 | (added word in bold)
Christ, the One empowering me

Original Text: τω ενδυναμουντι με (**the One empowering me**). This is the original wording according to four early MSS (ℵ* A B I), as well as D* 33 1739 it cop.

Textual Gap-filling: A variant reading adds Χριστω creating the rendering, "Christ, the One empowering me" in ℵ² [seventh century] D² (F G) Ψ Maj syr (so TR and KJV), by way of scribal gap-filling, wherein a scribe was influenced by 1 Timothy 1:12.

4:23
The word αμην (amen) is included in three early MSS (𝔓⁴⁶ ℵ A), as well as D Ψ 33 1739ᶜ Maj syr copᵇᵒ. The word is omitted in one early MS (B), as well as F G 1739* itᵇ copˢᵃ. The textual evidence casts doubts on the inclusion of "amen," as does the fact that "amen" was frequently added by scribes at the end of epistles. In fact, a final "amen" to an epistle is only certain in Galatians 6:18 and Jude 25.

Chapter Twelve

Colossians

Colossians
1:2 | (added words in bold)
God our Father **and the Lord Jesus Christ**

Original Text: θεου πατρος ημων (**God our Father**). This is the original wording according to the two earliest MSS ($\mathfrak{P}^{46vid}$ B), as well as D L Ψ 33 1739.

Textual Gap-filling: A variant reading adds και κυριου Ιησου Χριστου creating the rendering, "God our Father and Lord Jesus Christ" in four early MSS (ℵ A C I), as well as F G 075 Maj (so TR and KJV). Scribes were influenced by their reading of all of Paul's other epistles, which formed a horizon of expectation for this text and they made the addition accordingly (see Rom 1:7; 1 Cor 1:3; 2 Cor 1:2; Gal 1:3; Eph 1:2; Phil 1:2; 1 Thess 1:1; 2 Thess 1:1; 1 Tim 1:2; 2 Tim 1:2; Titus 1:4; Phm 3).

2:2
There are many variants added to the expression "mystery of God, Christ" (see below).

Original Text: του μυστηριου του θεου, Χριστου (**the mystery of God, Christ**). This is the original wording according to the two earliest MSS ($\mathfrak{P}^{46}$ B).

Textual Gap-filling: There are several variant readings: "the mystery of God, which is Christ" (D*), "the mystery of God" (D¹ H P), "the mystery of Christ" (81 1739), "the mystery of God, Father of Christ" (ℵ* A C 048ᵛⁱᵈ), "the mystery of God, even the Father of Christ" (ℵ² [seventh century] Ψ 0208), and "the mystery of God and of the Father and of Christ" (D² Maj; so KJV). Among the myriad variations, the testimony of the two earliest MSS (𝔓⁴⁶ B) is to be followed; Christ is God's mystery—now revealed.

2:18 | (added word in bold)
delving into things which he has **not** seen

Original Text: α εορακεν εμβατευων (**delving into things which he has seen**). This is the original wording according to four early MSS (𝔓⁴⁶ ℵ* A B), as well as D* F G 33 1739. Strong documentary support affirms that Paul was writing about "visions."
Textual Gap-filling: Other MSS add μη or ουκ (both mean "not")—in ℵ² [seventh century] C D¹ Ψ 075 0278 Maj (so TR and KJV), creating the reading "delving into things which he has not seen." Scribes thought this was what Paul meant—the heretics were talking about things they hadn't really seen or understood.

3:6 | (added words in bold)
God's anger comes against **the sons of disobedience.**

Original Text: ερχεται η οργη του θεου (**the anger of God comes**). This is the original wording according to the two earliest MSS (𝔓⁴⁶ B).
Textual Gap-filling: A variant adds επι τους υιους της απειθειας creating the rendering, "God's anger comes on the sons of disobedience" in four MSS (ℵ A C I), as well as D F G H Ψ 33 1739 Maj (so TR and KJV). This is scribal gap-filling, wherein Ephesians 5:6, a parallel verse, formed the horizon of expectation for certain scribes, and they filled the gap accordingly.

3:22 | (added words in bold)
obey your earthly masters **in everything you do**

Original Text: υπακουετε τοις κατα σαρκα κυριοις (**obey your earthly masters**). This is probably the original wording according to the earliest MS ($\mathfrak{P}^{46}$), as well as 075 0278.

Textual Gap-filling: A variant reading adds κατα παντα creating the rendering, "obey your earthly masters in everything you do" in four early MSS (ℵ A B C), as well as D F G 33 1739 Maj (so TR and KJV)—perhaps scribal gap-filling intended to indicate to what extent slaves should obey their masters.

4:18

The word αμην (amen) was added in several MSS (ℵ² D Ψ Maj; so TR and KJV) by way of scribal gap-filling. The addition was made in the interest of oral reading in the church.

Chapter Thirteen

First Thessalonians

First Thessalonians
1:1 | (added words in bold)
Grace to you and peace **from God our Father and the Lord Jesus Christ.**

Original Text: χαρις υμιν και ειρηνη (**grace to you and peace**). This is the original wording according to the two earliest MSS ($\mathfrak{P}^{46\text{vid}}$ B), as well as F G Ψ 0278.

Textual Gap-filling: A variant reading adds, απο θεου πατρος ημων και κυριου Ιησου Χριστου (from God our Father and the Lord Jesus Christ) in three early MSS (א A I), as well as (D) 33 Maj (so TR and KJV). This is scribal expansion influenced by the scribes' horizon of expectation wherein they have read the beginning of several epistles (Rom 1:7; 1 Cor 1:3; 2 Cor 1:2; Gal 1:3; Eph 1:2; Phil 1:2; 2 Thess 1:2; 1 Tim 1:2; 2 Tim 1:2; Titus 1:4), and then made the addition by way of scribal gap-filling.

5:28
The word αμην (amen) was added in several MSS (א A D[1] Ψ Maj; so TR and KJV) by way of scribal gap-filling. The addition was made in the interest of oral reading in the church.

Chapter Fourteen

Second Thessalonians

Second Thessalonians
1:1 | (added word in bold)
Lord Jesus **Christ**

Original Text: κυριω Ιησου (**Lord Jesus**). This is the reading in the earliest MS ($\mathfrak{P}^{30}$). (See Comfort & Barrett, *Text of Earliest NT Greek MSS*, 131, for reconstruction of $\mathfrak{P}^{30}$.)
Textual Gap-filling: All other MSS add Χριστω creating the rendering, "Lord Jesus Christ," probably by way of scribal expansion.

1:12 | (added word in bold)
the name of our Lord Jesus **Christ**

Original Text: το ονομα του κυριου ημων Ιησου (**the name of our Lord Jesus**). This is the reading in the two earliest MSS (א B), as well as D K L Ψ 0111.
Textual Gap-filling: A variant on the name adds Χριστου creating the rendering "Lord Jesus Christ" in A F G P 0278, by way of scribal gap-filling. The last words of the verse read, "the grace of our God and Lord, Jesus Christ." According to a grammatical rule, wherein one definite article governs two nouns joined by *kai* (known as the Granville Sharpe rule), "Jesus Christ" is identified as both "God" and "Lord" in the statement.

3:18

The word αμην (amen) was added in several MSS ($\aleph^2$ A D F G Ψ Maj; so TR and KJV) by way of scribal gap-filling. The addition was made in the interest of oral reading in the church.

Chapter Fifteen

First Timothy

First Timothy
1:17a | (added word in bold)
indestructible, invisible, **immortal**

Original Text: αφθαρτω αορατω (**indestructible, invisible**). This is the reading in the earliest MS (ℵ).

Textual Gap-filling: The word αθανατω (immortal) was added in F and G read, creating the rendering "indestructible, invisible, immortal." The Greek behind "indestructible" is αφθαρτος; it denotes that which cannot be corrupted and does not perish. Greek philosophers applied this characteristic to the soul (as opposed to the body). "Invisible" means that which cannot be seen with the mortal eye (*a* + *horatos*; cf. Col 1:15).

1:17b | (added word in bold)
the only **wise** God

Original Text: μονω θεω (**only God**). This is the original wording according to two early MSS (ℵ* A), as well as D* F G H* 33 1739 cop.

Textual Gap-filling: A variant reading adds σοφω, creating the rendering "the only wise God" in ℵ² [seventh century] D¹ Hᶜ Ψ Maj (so TR and KJV), by way of scribal expansion influenced by Romans 16:27.

The statement "he alone is God" (lit. "the only God") is distinctively Jewish (as opposed to the polytheism of the non-Jewish world). The adjective "wise" was added because Romans 16:27 formed a horizon of expectation, and the gap was filled accordingly.

3:16 | (added word in bold)
God was manifested in the flesh

Original Text: ος εφανερωθη εν σαρκι (**who was manifest in the flesh**). This is the original reading supported by the earliest MSS (**א*** A* C*), as well as F G 33.

Textual Gap-filling: Other MSS add θεος "God" (**א**c Ac C2 [sixth century] D2 Ψ 1739; so TR and KJV). The documentation evidence supporting "who" (or "he who") is very strong; many MSS were corrected to read "God"—clearly the result of scribal emendation. Obviously, the pronoun "who" refers to Jesus Christ, God incarnate.

6:21
Some MSS (**א**2 [seventh century] D1 Ψ 1739c Maj; so TR and KJV) add αμην (amen) at the end of the verse by way of scribal expansion, wherein the word enhances oral reading in church.

Chapter Sixteen

Second Timothy

Second Timothy
1:11 | (added words in bold)
teacher **of the Gentiles**

Original Text: διδασκαλος (**teacher**). This is the original wording according to three early MSS (ℵ* A I).
Textual Gap-filling: Several MSS expand the title to διδασκαλος εθνων "teacher of the Gentiles" in ℵ² [seventh century] C D F G Ψ 1739 Maj it syr cop (so TR and KJV) by way of scribal gap-filling, defining who Paul taught—namely, the Gentiles.

4:22a | (added words in bold)
the Lord **Jesus Christ**

Original Text: ο κυριος (**the Lord**). This is the original wording according to the earliest MS (ℵ*), as well as F G 33 1739.
Textual Gap-filling: Two variant readings are "Lord Jesus" (adding Ιησους) in A and "Lord Jesus Christ" (adding Ιησους Χριστος) in ℵ² [seventh century] C D Ψ Maj (so TR and KJV)—both the products of scribal gap-filling.

4:22b

Later MSS ($\aleph^2$ [seventh century] D Ψ 1739ᶜ Maj (so TR and KJV) add αμην (amen) at the end of the verse by way of scribal expansion; it is not included in the three earliest MSS ($\aleph$* A C), nor in F G 33 1739*.

Chapter Seventeen

Titus

Titus
2:7 | (added word in bold)
be serious, **incorruptible**

Original Text: σεμνοτητα (**serious**). This is the original wording according to the four earliest MSS ($\mathfrak{P}^{32vid}$ ℵ A C), as well as D* F G 33 1739.
Textual Gap-filling: A variant reading adds αφθαρσιαν creating the rendering "be serious, incorruptible" in D² Ψ Maj (so KJV), by way of scribal gap-filling influenced by 2 Timothy 1:10.

3:15
Some later MSS (ℵ² [seventh century] D¹ F G H Ψ 0278 Maj; so TR and KJV) add "amen" at the end of the verse by way of scribal expansion; it is not included in the three earliest MSS (ℵ* A C), nor in D* 048 33 1739. It was added in the interest of oral reading in church.

Chapter Eighteen

Philemon

Philemon
1:6 | (added word in bold)
Christ **Jesus**

Original Text: Χριστου (**Christ**). This is the original reading according to the three earliest MSS (א* A C), as well as 𝔓[61] 33.
Textual Gap-filling: A variant reading adds Ιησουν, creating the rendering "Christ Jesus" in א[2] [seventh century] D F G 1739 Maj by way of scribal gap-filling, expanding a divine name.

1:25
Several MSS (א C D[1] Ψ 0278 1739[c] Maj; so TR and KJV) add "amen" at the end of the verse by way of scribal expansion; it is not included in 𝔓[87] A D* 048[vid] 33 1739*. It was added in the interest of oral reading in church.

Chapter Nineteen

Hebrews

Hebrews
1:3 | (added words in bold)
by himself cleansed sins

Original Text: καθαρισμον των αμαρτιων (**cleansed sins**). This may be the original reading according to several early MSS (ℵ A B), as well as D¹ H* P Ψ 33.
Textual Gap-filling: Other MSS add δι εαυτου (by himself). This is the reading in the earliest MS ($\mathfrak{P}^{46}$), as well as D* Hᶜ 0243 0278 1739 Maj. The textual evidence is divided; either reading could be original. But if the reading of ℵ et al., is original, "by himself" is the product of natural gap-filling.

2:7 | (added words in bold)
crowned him with glory and honor, **and you set him over the work of your hands**

Original Text: δοξη και τιμη εστεφανωσας αυτον (**crowned him with glory and honor**). This is the original wording according to the two earliest MSS ($\mathfrak{P}^{46}$ B), as well as D² Maj.
Textual Gap-filling: A variant reading adds και κατεστησας αυτον επι τα εργα των χειρων σου creating the rendering, "crowned him

with glory and honor, and you set him over the works of your hands." This is added in three early MSS (א A C), as well as D* Ψ 33 1739 (so TR and KJV), by way of scribal gap-filling wherein the scribes were influenced by Psalm 8:7, the verse quoted here.

2:8 | (added words in bold)
he subjected all things **to him**

Original Text: υποταξαι τα παντα (**he subjected all things**). This is the original wording according to the two earliest MSS (𝔓⁴⁶ B).
Textual Gap-filling: Other MSS add αυτω, creating the rendering "he subjected all things to him" in א A C D Ψ 33 1739 Maj (so TR and KJV). This the product of natural scribal gap-filling.

3:2 | (added word in bold)
Moses was in his **entire** house

Original text: Μωυσης εν τω οικω αυτου (**Moses in his house**). This is the original wording according to the three earliest MSS (𝔓¹³ 𝔓⁴⁶vid B).
Textual Gap-filling: A variant reading adds ολω, creating the rendering, "Moses was in his entire house" in א A C D Ψ 33 1739 Maj (so TR and KJV), by way of scribal gap-filling wherein scribes were influenced by 3:5.

3:6 | (added words in bold)
we hold to our hope **firmly until the end**

Original Text: της ελπιδος κατασχωμεν (**we hold to our hope**). This is the original wording according to the three earliest MSS (𝔓¹³ 𝔓⁴⁶ B).
Textual Gap-filling: A variant reading adds μεχρι τελους βεβαιαν creating the rendering, "we hold to our hope firmly until the end" in three early MSS (א C), as well as D Ψ 33 1739 Maj (so TR and KJV), by way of scribal gap-filling wherein scribes were influenced by 3:14.

4:3 | (added word in bold)
for we have not entered into **the** rest

Original Text: εισερχομεθα γαρ εις καταπαυσιν (**for we have not entered into rest**). This is the original wording according to the three earliest MSS ($\mathfrak{P}^{13vid}$ $\mathfrak{P}^{46}$ B), as well as D*.

Textual Gap-filling: A variant reading is, "we have not entered into *the* rest" in three early MSS (ℵ A C), as well as D^1 Ψ 33 1739 Maj, in a scribal attempt to specify the rest.

7:28 | (added word in bold)
appoints **high** priests

Original Text: καθιστησιν ιερεις (**appoints priests**). This is probably the original reading according to two early MSS ($\mathfrak{P}^{46vid}$ I^{vid}), as well as D syr^p cop^{sa}.

Textual Gap-filling: A variant reading is καθιστησιν αρχιερεις "appoints high priests" in four early MSS (ℵ A B C), as well as Ψ 33 1739 (so TR and KJV). The manuscript evidence is divided; either reading could be original. But if the second reading is not original, it is the product of scribal gap-filling, wherein the scribes were influenced by the context of the chapter which speaks of high priests.

9:14 | (added words in bold)
worship the living **and true** God

Original Text: λατρευειν θεω ζωντι (**worship the living God**). This is the original wording according to three early MSS ($\mathfrak{P}^{46vid}$ ℵ B), as well as D 33 1739 Maj.

Textual Gap-filling: A variant adds και αληθινω creating the rendering "worship the living and true God" in A P 0278 by way of scribal gap-filling, wherein 1 Thessalonians 1:9 formed a horizon of expectation for certain scribes and they filled the gap accordingly.

10:9 | (added words in bold)
I have come, **O God**, to do your will

Original Text: ηκω του ποιησαι το θελημα σου (**I have come to**

do your will). This is the original wording according to four early MSS
($\mathfrak{P}^{46}$ $\aleph^*$ A C), as well as D Ψ 33.

Textual Gap-filling: A variant reading adds o θεος creating the rendering, "I have come, O God, to do your will" in $\aleph^2$ [seventh century]
0278^{vid} 1739 Maj (TR and KJV), by way of scribal assimilation to 10:7.

10:30 | (added words in bold)
and again **the Lord says**

Original Text: και παλιν (**and again**). This is the original wording ac-
cording to three early MSS ($\mathfrak{P}^{13vid}$ $\mathfrak{P}^{46}$ $\aleph^*$), as well as D* Ψ 33 1739.

Textual Gap-filling: A variant reading adds λεγει κυριος creating the
rendering, "and again the Lord says" in $\aleph^2$ [seventh century] A D^2 Maj
(so TR and KJV), by way of natural gap-filling.

11:37 | (added words in bold)
they were tested, they were sawn in two

Original Text: επρισθησαν (**they were sawn in two**). This is the
reading in the earliest MS ($\mathfrak{P}^{46}$), as well as syr^p cop^{sa}.

Textual Gap-filling: A variant adds επειρασθησαν in different orders:
(1) "they were tested, they were sawn in two" ($\aleph$ D* L P 048 33), and
(2) "they were sawn in two, they were tested" ($\mathfrak{P}^{13vid}$ A D^c Ψ 1739),
probably both the products of scribal gap-filling.

13:21 | (added words in bold)
the glory forever **and ever**

Original Text: η δοξα εις τους αιωνας (the glory forever). This is
the original wording according to the earliest MS ($\mathfrak{P}^{46}$), as well as C^3
[ninth century] D Ψ.

Textual Gap-filling: By adding των αιωνων the expression becomes
"the glory forever and ever" in three early MSS ($\aleph$ A C*), as well as 0243
0285 33 1739 Maj.

13:25 | Grace be with you all.
This is the original wording according to three early MSS ($\mathfrak{P}^{46}$ $\aleph^*$ I^vid),
as well as 33. Several MSS ($\aleph^2$ [seventh century] A C D H 1739 Maj; so
TR and KJV) add "amen" by way of scribal expansion.

Chapter Twenty

The Epistle of James

The Epistle of James
4:4 | (added words in bold)
adulterers and adulteresses

Original Text: μοιχαλιδες (**adulteresses**). This is the original word according to the four earliest MSS ($\mathfrak{P}^{100}$ ℵ* A B), as well as 33 1739.
Textual Gap-filling: A variant reading adds μοιχοι και creating the rendering "adulterers and adulteresses" in ℵ² [seventh century] P Ψ Maj (so TR and KJV, by way of scribal gap-filling attempting to be inclusive of males and females. The feminine "adulteresses" refers to any and all (whether male or female) who turn away from God and go after other gods.

5:19 | (added words in bold)
wanders from **the way of** the truth

Original Text: πλανηθη απο της αληθειας (**wanders from the truth**). The words "the truth" are original according to two early MSS (A B), as well as P 048^vid 1739 Maj.
Textual Gap-filling: Two variants add οδου (1) "the way" ($\mathfrak{P}^{74}$) and (2) "the way of the truth" (ℵ 33) by way of scribal gap-filling.

5:20

The word αμην (amen) is added in a few minuscules by way of scribal filling, in the interest of oral reading in church.

Chapter Twenty-One

The First Epistle of Peter

The First Epistle of Peter
3:7 | (added words in bold)
multifarious grace of **eternal** life

Original Text: χαριτος ζωης (**grace of life**). This is the original wording according to three early MSS ($\mathfrak{P}^{81\text{vid}}$ B C*), as well as P Ψ 33 1739 Maj. **Textual Gap-filling:** Two variant readings are "grace of eternal life" ($\mathfrak{P}^{72}$ adding αιωνιου), and "multifarious grace of life" (‭א‬ A C² [sixth century] adding ποικιλης). $\mathfrak{P}^{72}$ identifies the "life" as being "eternal," which it is, and ‭א‬ et al. adds an adjective ("multifarious") influenced by 4:10.

3:14 | (added words in bold)
do not fear their terror **or be afraid**

Original Text: φοβον αυτων μη φοβηθητε (**do not fear their terror**). This is the original wording according to the two earliest MSS ($\mathfrak{P}^{72}$ B). **Textual Gap-filling:** Scribes add μηδε ταραχθητε creating the rendering, "do not fear their terror or be afraid" (‭א‬ A C P Ψ 33 1739 Maj; so TR and KJV) by way of scribal gap-filling.

5:10 | (added word in bold)
glory in Christ **Jesus**

Original Text: δοξαν εν Χριστω (**glory in Christ**). This is probably the original reading according to three early MSS (𝕏 B 0206^vid).
Textual Gap-filling: The name is expanded to "Christ Jesus" in two early MSS (𝔓^72 A), as well as P Ψ 33 1739 Maj (so TR and KJV).

5:14 | Greet one another with a loving kiss.

The epistle ends here in the earliest MS (𝔓^72). Several MSS add ειρηνη υμιν πασιν τοις εν Χριστω (peace be to all who are in Christ) in 𝕏 [add "Jesus" after "Christ"] A B Ψ 33 1739 Maj, to which some MSS append "amen" (𝕏 P 1739^c Maj: so TR and KJV), by way of scribal gap-filling made in the interest of oral reading in church.

Chapter Twenty-Two

The Second Epistle of Peter

The Second Epistle of Peter
2:6 | (added words in bold)
he condemned them **to destruction**

Original text: κατεκρινεν (**he condemned [them]**). This is probably the original wording according to three early MSS (𝔓⁷²* B C*), as well as 1739.

Textual Gap-filling: Certain MSS add καταστροφη creating the rendering "he condemned them to destruction" (𝔓⁷²ᵐᵍ ℵ A C² [sixth century] Ψ 33 Maj so TR and KJV)—the result of scribal gap-filling.

3:18

The final word is "amen" in four early MSS (𝔓⁷² ℵ A C), as well as P Ψ 33 1739ᶜ Maj (so TR and KJV). It is omitted in B 1739*. It is likely the original epistle did not have "amen" as the final word. Scribes had a propensity for adding it to the end of the epistles in the interest of oral reading in church.

Chapter Twenty-Three

The First Epistle of John

The First Epistle of John
4:3 | (added words in bold)
not confessing Jesus **come in the flesh**

Original Text: μη ομολογει τον Ιησουν (**not confessing Jesus**). This is the original wording according to two early MSS (A B), as well as 1739.
Textual Gap-filling: A variant reading adds εν σαρκι εληλυθοτα, creating the rendering "not confessing Jesus come in the flesh" in one early MS (ℵ), as well as Ψ (33) Maj (so TR and KJV), by way of scribal gap-filling, wherein the previous verse (4:2) formed a horizon expectation for scribes and the gap was filled accordingly.

5:7–8 | (added words in bold)
[7] **So there are three testifying in heaven: the Father, the Word, and the Holy Spirit. And these three are one.** [8] And there are three that testify **on earth**: the Spirit, the water, and the blood, and these three are one.

Original Text: τρεις εισιν οι μαρτυρουντες το πνευμα και το υδωρ και το αιμα και οι τρεις εις το εν εισιν (**there are three witnesses—the Spirit, the water, and the blood—and all three are one**). This is the wording in the earliest MSS (ℵ A B), as well as Ψ, and several early versions (Syriac, Coptic, Armenian, Ethiopic, Old Latin).

Textual Gap-filling: Some late MSS ([61 629 in part] 88 221 429 636 918 2318) add εν τω ουρανω ο πατηρ ο λογος και το αγιον πνευμα και ουτοι οι τρεις εν εισιν and they add εν τη γη in the next verse, creating the rendering, "there are three testifying in heaven: the Father, the Word, and the Holy Spirit. And these three are one. And there are three that testify on earth: the Spirit, the water, and the blood, and these three are one." This expanded passage called the "heavenly witness" passage or *Comma Johanneum*, came from scribal gap-filling, a gloss on 5:8 which explained that the three elements (water, blood, and Spirit), symbolize the Trinity (the Father, the Word [Son], and the Spirit). The gloss showed up in the writings of Latin fathers in North Africa and Italy (as part of the text of the epistle) from the fifth century onward, and it found its way into more and more copies of the Latin Vulgate. (The original translation of Jerome did not include it.) "The heavenly witnesses" passage has not been found in the text of any Greek manuscript prior to the fourteenth century. Nonetheless, it was included in the Textus Receptus, and was translated in the KJV.

The passage as written by John has nothing to do with the Trinity, but with the three critical phases in Jesus' life where he was manifested as God-incarnate, the Son of God in human form. This was made evident at his baptism (= the water), his death (= the blood), and his resurrection (= the Spirit). At his baptism, the man Jesus was declared God's beloved Son (see Matt 3:16–17). At his crucifixion, a man spilling blood was recognized by others as "God's Son" (see Mark 15:39). In resurrection, he was designated as the Son of God in power (Rom 1:3–4). This trifold testimony is unified in one aspect: each event demonstrated that the man Jesus was the divine Son of God.

5:21

The word αμην (amen) was added by various scribes (P Maj; so TR and KJV) by way of scribal gap-filling in the interest of oral reading in church.

Chapter Twenty-Four

The Second Epistle of John

The Second Epistle of John
1:3 | (added words in bold)
the Lord Jesus Christ

Original Text: Ιησου Χριστου (**Jesus Christ**). This is the original reading according to three early MSS (A B 0232).
Textual Gap-filling: Certain scribes added κυριου, creating the rendering "Lord Jesus Christ" in one early MS (ℵ), as well as 𝔓³³ Maj (so TR and KJV), by way of scribal gap-filling, expanding the title.

1:13
The word αμην (amen) was added by various scribes (Maj; so TR and KJV) by way of scribal gap-filling in the interest of oral reading in church.

Chapter Twenty-Five

The Third Epistle of John

The Third Epistle of John
1:15
The word αμην (amen) was added by various scribes (L 614) by way of scribal gap-filling in the interest of oral reading in church.

Chapter Twenty-Six

The Epistle of Jude

The Epistle of Jude
1:22–23
There are many textual variants (see below).

Original Text: εκ πυρος αρπασατε διακρινομενους δε ελεειτε εν φοβος (**and snatch some from the fire, and show mercy with fear to others who have doubts**). This is the reading in the earliest MS ($\mathfrak{P}^{72}$).

Textual Gap-filling: There are several variants: (1) "and show mercy to some who have doubts—save them by snatching them from the fire; and to some show mercy with fear" (B); (2) "and have mercy on some, making a difference, and others, save with fear, pulling them out of the fire" (Maj; so KJV); (3) "and reprove some who have doubts [or, who dispute] and in fear save some from fire" (C*); (4) "and show mercy to some who have doubts [or, who dispute], and save some, snatching them from the fire, and to some show mercy with fear" (א); (5) "and reprove some who have doubts [or, who dispute], and save some, snatching them from the fire, and to some show mercy with fear" (A). The short reading in $\mathfrak{P}^{72}$ (which is nearly the same in B) could be original. If so, the other variants are scribal expansions.

Chapter Twenty-Seven

The Revelation of John

The Revelation of John
1:6 | (added words in bold)
forever **and ever**

Original Text: εις τους αιωνας (**forever**). This is the original wording according to two early MSS ($\mathfrak{P}^{18}$ A), as well as P.
Textual Gap-filling: A variant reading adds των αιωνων creating the rendering "forever and ever" in two early MSS (ℵ C), as well as Maj (so TR and KJV), by way of scribal gap-filling.

1:8 | (added words in bold)
the Alpha and the Omega, **the beginning and the end**

Original Text: το αλφα και το ω (**the Alpha and the Omega**). This is the original wording according to three early MSS (ℵ[1] A C).
Textual Gap-filling: A variant reading adds αρχη και τελος, creating the rendering, "the Alpha and Omega, the beginning and the end" according to ℵ[*,2] [seventh century] Maj[A] it cop[bo], by way of scribal gap-filling, wherein 21:6 and 22:13, parallel verses, formed a horizon of expectation for the reading of 1:8 and the gap was filled accordingly. The additional words were put into the TR, followed by the KJV.

1:18 | (added word in bold)
forever and ever, **amen**

Original Text: εις τους αιωνας των αιωνων (**for ever and ever**). This is the original wording according to four early MSS ($\mathfrak{P}^{98vid}$ ℵ* A C), as well as P.
Textual Gap-filling: A variant reading adds αμην, creating the rendering, "forever and ever, amen" in ℵ¹ Maj (so TR and KJV), by way of scribal gap-filling, influenced by oral reading.

11:19 | (added words in bold)
the ark of the covenant **of the Lord [God]**

Original Text: η κιβωτος της διαθηκης (**the ark of the covenant**). This is the original wording according to three early MSS ($\mathfrak{P}^{115vid}$ A C).
Textual Gap-filling: Two variant readings are "the ark of the covenant of the Lord" in one early MS ($\mathfrak{P}^{47}$ adding κυριου), as well as Maj^K, and "the ark of the covenant of God" in one early MS (ℵ adding θεου), both the product of scribal gap-filling.

18:2 | (added words in bold)
a prison of every wicked bird **and a prison of detestable creatures**

Original Text: και φυλακη παντος ορνεου ακαθαρτου (**and a prison of every wicked bird**). This is the original wording according to two early MSS (ℵ C), as well as Maj.
Textual Gap-filling: A variant reading adds και φυλακη παντος θηριου ακαθαρτου, creating the rendering "and a prison of every wicked bird and a prison of detestable creatures" in one early MS (A) by way of scribal expansion.

20:5
This is the first resurrection. **The rest of the dead did not live again until the thousand years were completed.**

Original Text: αυτη η αναστασις η πρωτη (**this is the first resurrection**). This is the reading in one early MS (א), as well as Maj[K].

Textual Gap-filling: A variant reading in two early MSS (A C) is οι λοιποι των νεκρων ουκ εζησαν αχρι τελεσθη τα χιλια ετη (**the rest of the dead did not come to life until the thousand years were finished**). The omission in א may have been accidental; but if intentional, it eliminates the problem of explaining how certain Christians (i.e., the martyrs of 20:4) are allowed to participate in the first resurrection and the millennial kingdom, while others (i.e., those who are not martyrs) have to wait until after the millennium to experience resurrection. If the reading in א is original, then the longer text could be a scribal gloss that found its way into the text.

22:21a | (added words in bold)
the grace of the Lord Jesus be with all **the saints**

Original Text: η χαρις του κυριου Ιησου μετα παντων (**the grace of the Lord Jesus be with all**). This is the reading in one early MS (א). **Scribal Gap-filling:** Two variant readings are, "the grace of the Lord Jesus be with all the saints" in Maj syr cop (adding των αγιων), and "the grace of the Lord Jesus be with you all" in A (adding υμων)—probably both scribal expansions.

22:21b
The word αμην (amen) is found in one early MS (א), as well as Maj syr cop (so TR and KJV), but omitted in one early MS (A) and other MSS. It is probably a scribal addition influenced by oral reading in church.

Select Bibliography

The following bibliography pertains to volumes I used in preparing the book.

Aland, Kurt, and Barbara Aland. 1987. *The Text of the New Testament*. Grand Rapids: Eerdmans.

Aland, Kurt, Barbara Aland, J. Karavidopoulos, C. Martini, and B. Metzger. 2012. *Novum Testamentum Graece* (28th ed.). Stuttgart: Deutsche Bibelgesellschaft.

_____. 1993. *The Greek New Testament* (4th rev. ed.). Stuttgart: Deutsche Bibelgesellschaft.

Bell, Harold I., and T. C. Skeat. 1935. *Fragments of an Unknown Gospel and Other Early Christian Papyri*. London: British Library.

Bruce, F. F. 1985. *The Letter of Paul to the Romans*, 2nd ed. Grand Rapids: Eerdmans.

_____. 1989. *The Canon of Scripture*. Grand Rapids: Eerdmans.

Colwell, E. 1965. "Scribal Habits in Early Papyri: A Study in the Corruption of the Text." In *The Bible in Modern Scholarship*, edited by J. P. Hyatt, 370–389. Nashville: Abingdon.

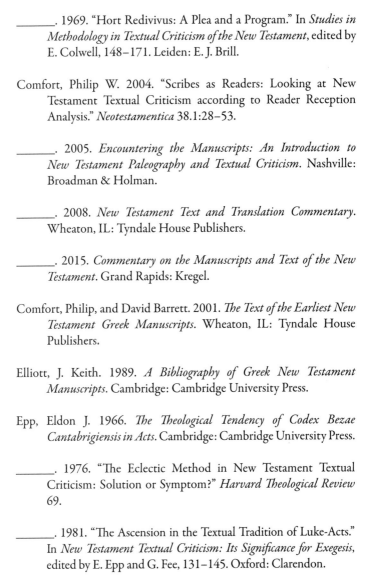

_____. 1969. "Hort Redivivus: A Plea and a Program." In *Studies in Methodology in Textual Criticism of the New Testament*, edited by E. Colwell, 148–171. Leiden: E. J. Brill.

Comfort, Philip W. 2004. "Scribes as Readers: Looking at New Testament Textual Criticism according to Reader Reception Analysis." *Neotestamentica* 38.1:28–53.

_____. 2005. *Encountering the Manuscripts: An Introduction to New Testament Paleography and Textual Criticism*. Nashville: Broadman & Holman.

_____. 2008. *New Testament Text and Translation Commentary*. Wheaton, IL: Tyndale House Publishers.

_____. 2015. *Commentary on the Manuscripts and Text of the New Testament*. Grand Rapids: Kregel.

Comfort, Philip, and David Barrett. 2001. *The Text of the Earliest New Testament Greek Manuscripts*. Wheaton, IL: Tyndale House Publishers.

Elliott, J. Keith. 1989. *A Bibliography of Greek New Testament Manuscripts*. Cambridge: Cambridge University Press.

Epp, Eldon J. 1966. *The Theological Tendency of Codex Bezae Cantabrigiensis in Acts*. Cambridge: Cambridge University Press.

_____. 1976. "The Eclectic Method in New Testament Textual Criticism: Solution or Symptom?" *Harvard Theological Review* 69.

_____. 1981. "The Ascension in the Textual Tradition of Luke-Acts." In *New Testament Textual Criticism: Its Significance for Exegesis*, edited by E. Epp and G. Fee, 131–145. Oxford: Clarendon.

Farmer, William. 1974. *The Last Twelve Verses of Mark*. Cambridge: Cambridge University Press.

Fee, Gordon. 1974. "$\mathfrak{P}^{75}$, $\mathfrak{P}^{66}$, and Origen: The Myth of the Early Textual Recension in Alexandria." In *New Dimensions in New Testament Study*, edited by R. Longenecker and M. Tenney, 19–45. Grand Rapids: Zondervan.

Gadamer, Hans-Georg. 1976. *Philosophical Hermeneutics*. Translated and edited by David E. Linge. Berkeley: University of California Press.

Gamble, Harry. 1977. *The Textual History of the Letter to the Romans*. Studies and Documents 42. Grand Rapids: Eerdmans.

_____. 1995. *Books and Readers in the Early Church*. New Haven, CT: Yale University Press.

Holmes, Michael. 2002. "The Case for Reasoned Eclecticism." In *Rethinking New Testament Textual Criticism*, edited by D. Black, 77–100. Grand Rapids: Baker.

Iser, Wolfgang. 1978. *The Act of Reading*. Baltimore: Johns Hopkins University Press.

Metzger, Bruce. 1977. *The Early Versions of the New Testament*. Oxford: Clarendon.

_____. 1992. *The Text of the New Testament: Its Transmission, Corruption, and Restoration*, 3rd ed. Oxford: Oxford University Press.

_____. 1994. *A Textual Commentary on the Greek New Testament* [abbreviated as TCGNT], 2nd ed. New York: United Bible Societies.

Select Bibliography

Porter, Calvin. 1962. "Papyrus Bodmer XV ($\mathfrak{P}^{75}$) and the Text of Codex Vaticanus." *Journal of Biblical Literature* 81:363–376.

Richards, E. Randolph. 1991. *The Secretary in the Letters of Paul.* Tubingen: J. C. B. Mohr.

Skeat, T. C. 1938. "The Lilies of the Field." *Zeitschrift fur die neutestamentliche Wissenschaft* 37:211–214.

_____. 1997. "The Oldest Manuscript of the Four Gospels?" *New Testament Studies* 43:1–34.

Tregelles, Samuel P. 1854. *An Account of the Printed Text of the Greek New Testament.* London: Samuel Bagster and Sons.

Westcott, Brooke F., and Fenton J. A. Hort. 1881. *The New Testament in the Original Greek.* Cambridge: Macmillan.

_____. 1882. *The New Testament in the Original Greek, Introduction and Appendix.* New York: Harper & Brothers.